WIND TOWERS

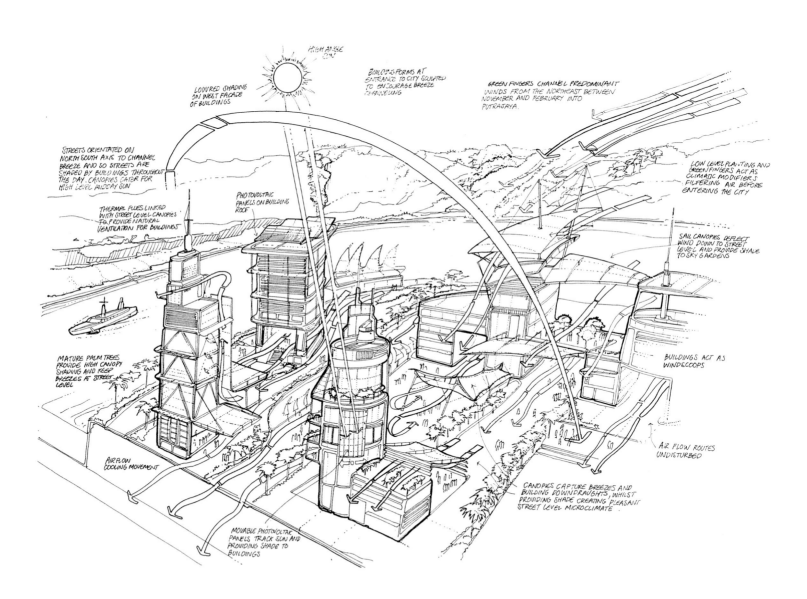

HIGH ANGLE SUN

LOUVRED SHADING ON WEST FACADE OF BUILDINGS

BUILDING FORMS AT ENTRANCE TO CITY SCULPTED TO ENCOURAGE BREEZE CHANNELLING

GREEN FINGERS CHANNEL PREDOMINANT WINDS FROM THE NORTHEAST BETWEEN NOVEMBER AND FEBRUARY INTO PUTRAJAYA.

STREETS ORIENTATED ON NORTH SOUTH AXIS TO CHANNEL BREEZE AND SO STREETS ARE SHADED BY BUILDINGS THROUGHOUT THE DAY. CANOPIES CATER FOR HIGH LEVEL MIDDAY SUN

LOW LEVEL PLANTING AND GREEN FINGERS ACT AS CLIMATIC MODIFIERS FILTERING AIR BEFORE ENTERING THE CITY

PHOTOVOLTAIC PANELS ON BUILDING ROOF

THERMAL FLUES LINKED WITH STREET LEVEL CANOPIES TO PROVIDE NATURAL VENTILATION FOR BUILDINGS

SAIL CANOPIES REFLECT WIND DOWN TO STREET LEVEL AND PROVIDE SHADE TO SKY GARDENS

MATURE PALM TREES PROVIDE HIGH CANOPY SHADING AND KEEP BREEZES AT STREET LEVEL

BUILDINGS ACT AS WINDSCOOPS

AIR FLOW COOLING MOVEMENT

AIR FLOW ROUTES UNDISTURBED

MOVABLE PHOTOVOLTAIC PANELS TRACK SUN AND PROVIDING SHADE TO BUILDINGS

CANOPIES CAPTURE BREEZES AND BUILDING DOWNDRAUGHTS, WHILST PROVIDING SHADE CREATING PLEASANT STREET LEVEL MICROCLIMATE

WIND TOWERS

BATTLE McCARTHY CONSULTING ENGINEERS

DETAIL IN BUILDING

A.D. ACADEMY EDITIONS

Cover: Bluewater Shopping Centre, Kent, UK
Page 2: Putrajaya core island area, Malaysia

First published in Great Britain in 1999 by
ACADEMY EDITIONS

A division of
JOHN WILEY & SONS
Baffins Lane
Chichester
West Sussex PO19 1UD

ISBN 0-471-98087-0

Other Wiley Editorial Offices
New York • Weinheim • Brisbane • Singapore • Toronto

Printed and bound in Italy

CONTENTS

PREFACE

Morphology is not only the study of material things and the forms of material things, but its dynamical aspects in terms of force, of the operation of energy.

D'Arcy Thompson, *On Growth and Form*, 1942

Over the years, there has been an increasing need for a better understanding of wind behaviour. As structures become larger and lighter, the effects and behaviour of wind on and around them become more noticeable. The expansion of the aeronautical industry has provided a source for more accurate wind data, as have airflow-testing facilities, developed by aeronautical engineers. This increased understanding of air flow around objects, together with the available wind data measured at each airport, has provided the basis for the rejuvenation of 'wind-building engineering'.

The technology developed to test large, supersonic aircraft such as Concorde in the 1960s created a new area of co-operation between the aeronautical industry and the construction industry. More detailed studies of the effects of wind loads upon buildings could be undertaken and wind-tunnel testing became the design tool to predict and address the effects of wind on new buildings and external spaces. This analysis primarily concerned architects, structural engineers and aeronautical engineers, looking at ways of reducing the negative aspects of wind loading by producing more aerodynamic buildings.

This collaboration has now moved on to the study of ways of using the wind surrounding the building as a means of driving ventilation. Those involved have sought a design tool that can analyse the movement of air through the building in order to ventilate it more effectively. Again, wind-tunnel testing has proved a primary source for understanding air movement within the building. Further developments in the aeronautical industry, such as computational fluid dynamic analysis programmes, are also now being used within the construction industry.

The engineering of wind for buildings has been extended to ventilating modern commercial developments that will transform the built environment in a new era of aerodynamic architecture.

fig 1

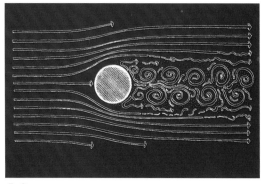

fig 2

fig 1 Cigarette smoke moving from laminar flow to turbulent flow.
fig 2 Turbulent flow in the wake of a cylinder in water.

Battle McCarthy Consulting Engineers, in collaboration with Imperial College, London (under the Department of the Environment's 'Partners in Technology' programme), has carried out extensive research into the use of wind energy for ventilating a wide range of buildings. Physical models of buildings with both wind towers and wind scoops and computer models (computational fluid dynamic analysis) were tested in a wind tunnel. The results provided a thorough understanding of the wind forces surrounding the building, and of how best to harness these forces. A calculation method was then developed to enable the user to determine the necessary height, diameter and position of wind towers and scoops to provide the required ventilation.[1]

fig 3

fig 4   fig 5

1 The results of the wind-tunnel testing, along with the calculation method can be found in *Wind Towers: the design of wind driven naturally ventilated buildings – the Calculation Method,* a Battle McCarthy Consulting Engineers project in collaboration with the Aeronautical Department of Imperial College, London, and partially funded by the Department of Environment 'Partners in Technology 1996'. Copies are available from: Battle McCarthy, 57 Poland Street, London W1V 3DF.

fig 3 Illustration of air drawn upwards through floor plates within the atrium of a tower.
fig 4 Flow patterns of a cylinder through still water.
fig 5 Flow patterns of a cylinder through waves.

INTRODUCTION

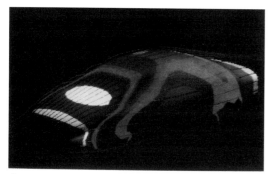

fig 6

fig 7

fig 6 and fig 8 The modern car is designed to create the least resistance to wind in order to increase performance. The objective when designing buildings with wind towers, however, is to create a resistance to the wind in order to utilise its energy.

fig 7 Ionica Headquarters Building, Cambridge, UK.

Even the earliest buildings were designed to provide shelter from the elements and protection from unwanted intruders. Traditionally, they reflected elements of the local environment, such as the materials available and the prevailing climate, though social, economic and cultural aspects have also shaped the built environment. The igloo, for example, is perfectly adapted to utilise to the best advantage the benefits of the freezing arctic conditions, and the adobe mud hut creates a thermally heavy-weight structure to minimise internal temperature swings.

Wind is a powerful force that should be harnessed and harvested to maximise its potential positive contribution to the built environment. In cold climates, wind has traditionally been viewed as a negative force, and buildings have been located and designed to minimise its effect. Today's architects are using natural forces positively, utilising the free energy available from the environment instead of creating an environmental barrier behind which we can cocoon ourselves within an artificial internal climate.

Buildings need to be ventilated throughout the year in order to maintain a level of fresh air. In the winter, ventilation should be minimised to reduce heat loss, but it should be maximised in the summer to optimise the human evaporative cooling process. Designers need to consider minimising the heat gains in a building to provide thermal comfort during the summer, as well as passive cooling. Strategies to minimise heat gain include shading, orientation, vegetation, insulation, daylight, and controllability.

Rather than concentrating on these issues, however, this book looks at techniques using natural forces such as the wind to cool a building – a well-designed structure that minimises heat gains and utilises passive cooling by means of wind-driven ventilation will require little or no mechanical ventilation. *Wind Towers* addresses the concept of providing controllable natural ventilation in a building by means of wind towers and/or wind scoops.

There is often confusion between wind towers and solar chimneys. Wind towers rely on the pressure difference over the building and across the device to drive air through the structure. Solar chimneys depend on stack effect for this, but it is a very weak force and cannot move air quickly. The stack effect will only exhaust air if the indoor temperature difference is greater than the outdoor one between the vertical openings, so solar chimneys are often glazed to increase solar gain and air movement.

This book deals solely with wind-driven devices, which have a number of advantages over solar chimneys. The correct positioning of the wind towers/scoops allows a smaller diameter of chimney than that required for stack effects alone. Wind-driven ventilation is also particularly suitable in temperate zones, where a relatively strong prevailing wind may be relied upon during the summer.

fig 8

PRESSURE AND WINDS

January

July

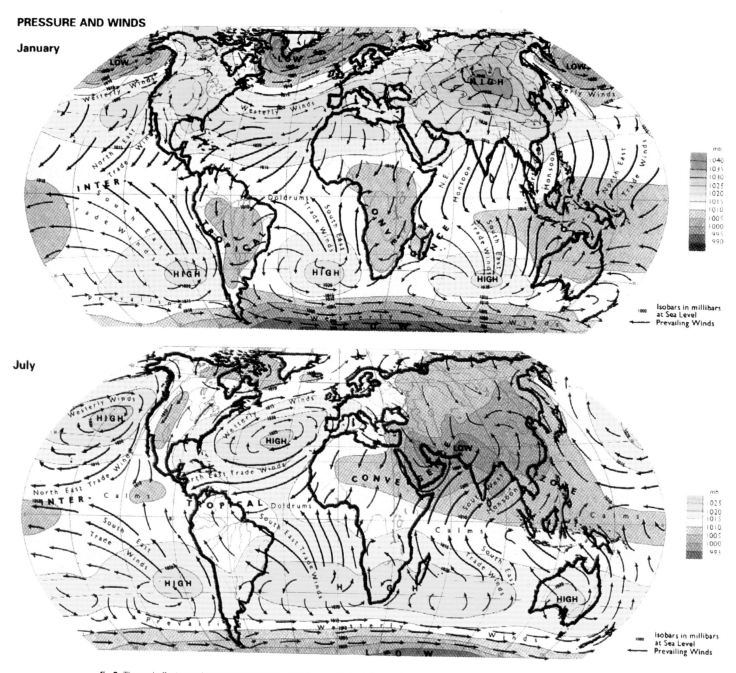

fig 9 Thermal effects produce a pressure differential that results in air flowing from the higher to the lower air-pressure region.
Cartography by Philip's © George Philip Ltd

CLIMATE AND THERMAL CONTROL

Architecture is increasingly being designed to utilise the free energy available from the environment, with the result that climatic forces are more and more responsible for shaping a new generation of structures. A diverse number of building types for which air-conditioning had previously been considered necessary, due to denser occupancy and high internal heat gains, are now being developed using natural ventilation as their primary source of ventilation. Reliance on air-conditioning has brought with it high energy consumption costs, as well as environmental implications. In the future, will we be able to afford to ventilate buildings by mechanical means alone?

Buildings account for approximately 50 per cent of the energy used in Europe, and are responsible for 30 to 40 per cent of carbon dioxide production. A major proportion of the energy consumed by buildings is the result of air-conditioning and therefore natural ventilation must be seen as a principal environmental building issue. Simple, traditional alternatives to air-conditioning need to be developed at an early stage of the design process in order to create low-energy, low-maintenance buildings of high environmental quality.

Naturally ventilating a building by means of wind towers or wind scoops provides increased reliability and control compared with cross-ventilation. The area of openings can be reduced, allowing the implementation of night-time cooling in the summer, and the means for heat recovery in the winter. However, natural ventilation may not be adequate to maintain satisfactory human-comfort requirements during peak summer periods in buildings with high internal heat gains. The return to full mechanical sealed buildings can be avoided by adopting a hybrid system using both natural and mechanical ventilation. During peak conditions, mechanical displacement ventilation will supply cool air at low level with extract air exhausted via the wind tower. To reduce heat loss during the winter, the mechanical ventilation system will also provide warm supply air, pre-heated by exhaust air via a heat exchanger. This is commonly known as a mixed-mode solution, whereby natural ventilation throughout the mid-season period (approximately 70 per cent of the year) provides major energy savings, and mechanical ventilation systems are operated only during extreme conditions. The new breed of low-energy, high-efficiency buildings with reduced running and maintenance costs and lower carbon dioxide emissions, which allow occupants a high level of control over their environment while enabling contact with the external environment, will form the architecture of the millennium.

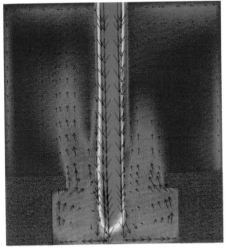

fig 10

fig 10 Computational Fluid Dynamic analysis of air flow through a wind scoop.

CLIMATE

Weather and climatic forces are products of solar radiation. The atmosphere of the earth absorbs solar energy, which in turn warms the planet's surface. The air close to the surface is heated and rises, creating low pressure. As the earth is not heated evenly, pockets of relatively high and low pressures are formed over its surface and wind is a direct consequence of this pressure differential, as air is moved from areas of high pressure to areas of low pressure.

Wind

Wind is a major design factor for architects. It greatly influences thermal comfort, modifying the heat exchange of a building envelope both in terms of convection and infiltration of air into the building. Understanding the nature of wind, and in particular how site wind conditions will affect a building proposal, is crucial if a construction is to be environmentally successful.

Local conditions to a large extent determine wind velocities, directions and temperatures. Information about these, and how they vary with seasonal changes, must be obtained if design issues are to be handled properly. The local Met Office or weather station usually compiles this type of weather data.

Most areas of the world have a prevailing wind, but this does not mean that these conditions occur all year round. It is likely that wind directions will vary according to season and the prevailing temperature. The Mistral in the south of France, for example, and the Sirocco in southern Italy, blow only at a certain time of year.

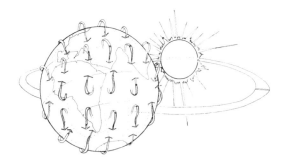

fig 11

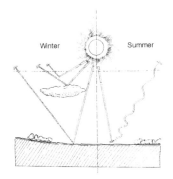

fig 12

fig 11 Different surfaces of the earth receive a varying degree of sunshine. The equator receives more than the poles, generating a global north-south flow of air. The rotation of the earth also creates north-south air currents by an effect known as the Coriolis force.

fig 12 Global convection currents affect seasonal change. Cloudy conditions block solar radiation, making temperature changes moderate. The more extreme temperature changes in summer strengthen prevailing winds.

fig 13 (opposite) World wind resource.

WORLD-WIDE WIND ENERGY RESOURCE DISTRIBUTION ESTIMATES

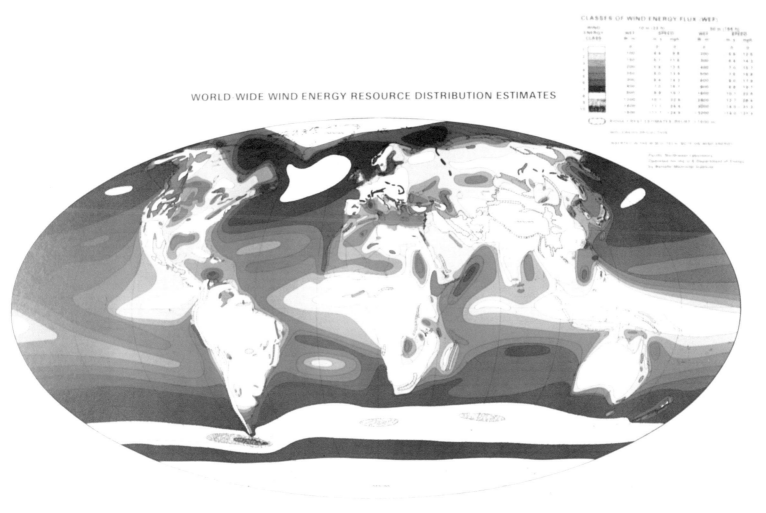

fig 13

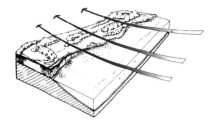

fig 14a

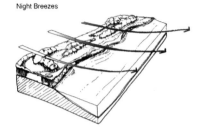

fig 14b

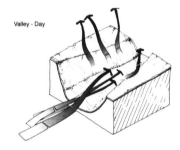

fig 14c

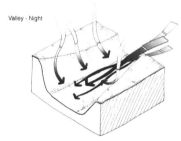

fig 14d

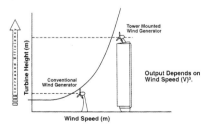

fig 15

MICROCLIMATE

If a building is to relate to and gain from its environment, it is important to understand regional weather patterns, but the microclimate of the area must also be carefully examined. The following factors can alter the macroclimate to produce a quite different microclimate:

• *Time of day* Day and night will produce two quite different conditions, sometimes reversing the direction of the prevailing wind. This is particularly the case in mountainous regions, where air will rise up a mountain during the day and fall during the night. Large bodies of water can also have the effect of reversing the wind flow as day turns to night.

• *Vegetation and soil type* Vegetation can produce enclosed conditions, either altering or reducing the wind speed or direction. The heat capacity, colour and water content of soil will affect the amount of heat absorption and therefore the ground temperature. This can have a significant effect on the microclimate because the ground temperature influences pressure systems.

• *Man-made structures* The built environment can significantly alter a microclimate. Overall, wind speed will be 25 per cent lower in built-up areas, though very high local wind speeds can occur due to urban canyons (buildings and streets that channel wind flow).

• *Topography* Generally, wind speeds will increase with altitude. The steeper the slope of land, the faster the temperature will drop at night, and this will alter the wind direction. The topography of the earth's surface has a major effect on microclimate, diverting or blocking winds. South-facing slopes, which receive more sunlight and are protected from cold north winds, are therefore more desirable than north-facing slopes.

• *Proximity to bodies of water* The proximity of land to a water mass will create air currents. Water has a high heat capacity and therefore a large water mass will not absorb heat as quickly, but will retain it longer than a similar area of land mass. Temperature changes over water therefore tend to be more moderate and produce a different pressure system from that over land. This pressure difference can generate daily alternating land and sea breezes.

There are many complex climatic factors that determine the direction and speed of the wind. However, when designing wind towers it is particularly important to take into consideration the fact that hot days induce winds, for the air movement through the building must be at its most effective during the hottest conditions.

fig 14a Day shore breezes. During the day, land is warmer than the sea, from which it draws air.
fig 14b Night shore breezes. At night, the sea is warmer than the land, from which it draws air.
fig 14c Valley – day Air is drawn up the mountain from the valley during the day.
fig 14d Valley – night. Cool air falls at night from the mountain to the valley.
fig 15 The efficiency of wind generation.

THERMAL COMFORT

Thermal comfort is a condition of both physical and mental well-being, and designers are responsible for providing an internal climatic environment that can produce it. The ventilation of a building is directly related to thermal comfort. By increasing the air velocity, the comfort zone shifts to a higher temperature. This means that occupants of the building will feel more comfortable, even though the building is not actually being cooled.

One of the most important factors of thermal comfort is whether the building's skin is sealed (ie whether it is possible to open windows). In an air-conditioned building, occupants will expect a tight temperature regime, but if windows can be opened they can exert more individual control on their environment. A recent survey suggests that 90 per cent of occupants prefer direct climatic control of the external environment to adjusting air-conditioning thermostats, where the change in local environment is not immediately apparent, and building agents are finding that there is an increasing demand for buildings with openable windows.

fig 16a

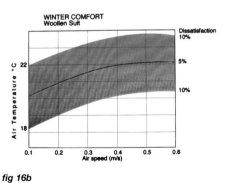

fig 16b

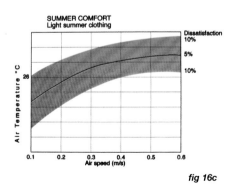

fig 16c

figs 16a, b, c Acceptable air temperature will increase as air speed increases. This reaches a limit at 0.8 m/s when air movement becomes uncomfortable.

15

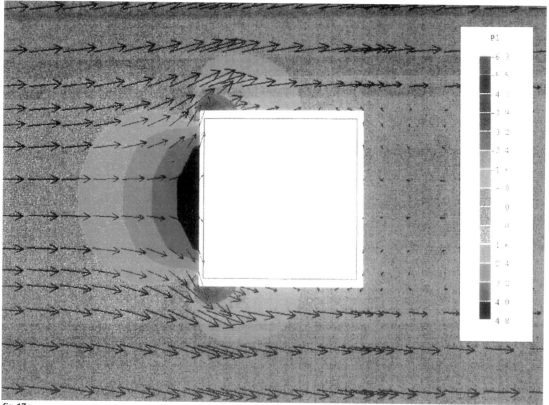

fig 17a

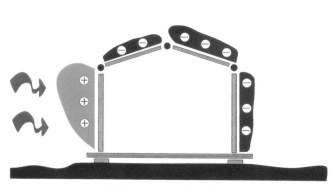

Wind pressure around building

fig 17b

Wind pressure around building

fig 17c

figs 17a, b, c As the wind hits an object in its path, the air molecules compress, becoming denser. As the air passes the the object, it accelerates, becoming less dense and generating a negative pressure or suction.

NATURAL AND WIND-DRIVEN VENTILATION

An understanding of the nature of wind and the pressure it will exert on a building is crucial for architects or designers utilising available wind energy. A building in the path of an air stream will produce a natural pressure difference: as air molecules are compressed, they increase pressure, and as they are dispersed, they decrease it. Natural ventilation is achieved by exploiting the pressure differences surrounding the building by placing inlets in areas of positive pressure and locating a wind tower in areas of negative pressure. The pressure differences between the inlet and the outlet locations provide the power to force the air through the building. A complex building in a complex environment will necessitate extreme care in choosing the size and location of the inlets and outlets.

A building in a wind path causes the air speed to decrease from 'free-stream air velocity' to 'still air' immediately adjacent to the windward wall. This reduction in dynamic pressure results in an increase in static pressure. Conversely, the air flowing round the sides and over the top of a building is accelerated because there is a smaller cross-sectional area for the air to flow through. The increase in velocity leads to a reduction in static pressure. With atmospheric pressure as a datum, this will be a negative pressure or suction.

NATURAL VENTILATION

Natural ventilation is achieved by making use of the natural pressure differences surrounding a building, caused by the wind and stack effect (as described above). Air movement within the building may also depend on buoyancy (thermal forces). There will always be periods of calm when the wind speed is ineffectual, although these do not generally occur during hot weather. In these situations, buoyancy forces act alone. Natural ventilation is dependent on three climatic phenomena: wind velocity, wind direction and temperature difference.

1. Wind velocity

The direction of the wind and its velocity over the building create a pressure field around the building. It is therefore important that the wind tower or wind scoop is positioned to maximise the pressure differential between the inlet and the extract. This will increase the efficiency of the ventilation scheme, allowing reduced opening areas. Pressure differential

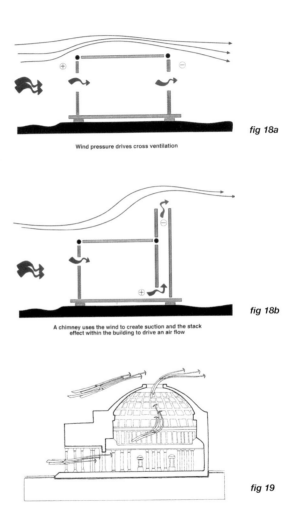

fig 18a

Wind pressure drives cross ventilation

fig 18b

A chimney uses the wind to create suction and the stack effect within the building to drive an air flow

fig 19

figs 18a, b Wind towers optimise pressure differences created by the wind, allowing reduced opening sizes and creating more controllable ventilation.
fig 19 The Pantheon in Rome, built by Agrippa in 27BC and rebuilt by Hadrian in 120–124AD uses wind-driven ventilation.

17

around the building will always be the predominant factor influencing natural ventilation, but this is reliant on the velocity of the wind. If this drops below a certain level, only then will stack effect (buoyancy) have any real bearing on the rate of ventilation. Wind ventilation is not effective unless wind speed is in excess of 2.5m/s; the average in the UK is 4.5 m/s.

2. Wind direction

The manner in which air passes through a building is fundamentally dependent on the direction of the wind. As the wind moves over the building it creates a varying positive and negative pressure field. Air will then flow from the positive pressure zones to the negative. It is important to note that as wind direction varies on a daily and seasonal basis, the pressure field around the building will also alter. An opening may therefore change from a positive pressure to a negative pressure from one day (or season) to the next.

3. Temperature differences

As the temperature increases, the density of air decreases and the air consequently rises. Temperature differences between the inside and outside of the building, and between different areas of the building, create pressure differences and, subsequently, air movement. This is known as 'stack effect'. A natural ventilation system should therefore also be designed to promote air buoyancy. It is desirable for the wind to apply its force in the same direction as the buoyancy force to avoid a condition in which the two forces cancel each other out. Buoyancy effects will, however, be exceeded by wind-generated pressures for wind speeds over 2.5 m/s.

The range of wind speeds and directions occurring within the built environment means that achieving a satisfactory natural ventilation system for a complex building in a complex environment can sometimes only be proved by wind-tunnel testing. Once the pressure at all potential locations for inlets and outlets has been measured, it is possible to determine the best locations for openings to provide natural ventilation.

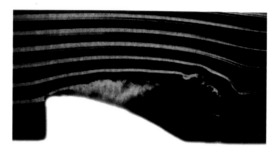

figs 20a, b Wind-tunnel testing of scale model to assess the performance of wind.

fig 20a

fig 20b

WIND-DRIVEN VENTILATION

Wind flowing around and across a building drives natural ventilation, and can be harnessed in a number of ways. Wind towers can be used to draw air out of the building, subsequently encouraging a natural air flow. Wind scoops can collect and deliver external air to the building, and a combination of wind towers and wind scoops can provide a natural form of air delivery and extraction.

Wind towers

The simplest design for a wind tower is a vertical construct that projects above its surroundings and has an open top. This will ensure negative pressure and provide suction in all wind directions. If the ingress of rain is a problem, a cover can be placed above the top. Alternatively, an oast wind tower (L-bend) will reduce the effect of interference at the opening and provide a greater degree of protection from the weather. However, if an oast tower is to work in all wind directions, it must be omnidirectional and turn away from the wind, which obviously carries cost and maintenance implications. A number of other devices can be incorporated into the basic chimney design to create a greater negative pressure around the opening, but generally these must also be omnidirectional.

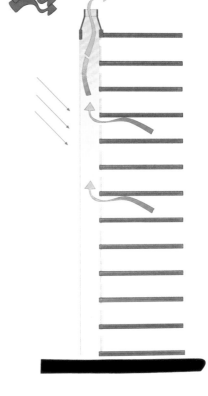

fig 21

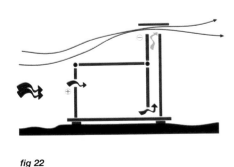

fig 22

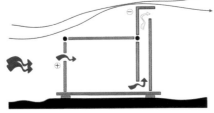

fig 23

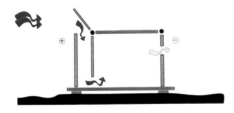

fig 24

fig 25

fig 21 Buildings that are naturally ventilated through windows are restricted to certain plan depths. Single-sided ventilation is effective for a depth of 6m, and conventional ventilation is effective to 15m depth. In contrast, wind towers and wind scoops provide considerable flexibility. Opening-area requirements are reduced and shorter ventilation routes may be available due to the position of the devices.
fig 22 Wind tower design. Wind creates suction to draw air through the building.
fig 23 Oast wind tower.
fig 24 Wind scoop directs wind through the building.
fig 25 Wind scoop placed some distance from the building. Air supplied is via earth tubes, which pre-cool air supply.

Wind scoops

Wind scoops are designed to 'catch' the wind and direct fresh air into the building. To operate effectively they must be omnidirectional, turning into the wind. Fixed wind scoops quickly become ineffective if the wind is not directed head-on to the scoop, and will even work in reverse (acting as an oast wind tower). Wind scoops are particularly effective when supplying large, open spaces such as atria, allowing cooler air to drop and mix within the space. They can be mounted on the roofs of buildings or placed in the landscape some distance away, the supply air being brought in via earth tubes.

Wind towers and wind scoops

Wind scoops can be used in combination with wind towers to create a system by which cool air is provided by wind scoops and warm air is then extracted via wind towers. By collecting and extracting air at high level, rather than through the facades, there will be a greater pressure differential between the devices, producing more air flow through the building. Natural ventilation by means of a combination of wind towers and wind scoops can either be via two separate devices, or a single device with both inlet and extract.

Again, the wind scoop should be omnidirectional, and if a combined device is used, an omnidirectional wind tower can also be employed. An alternative device may be installed, however, to eliminate the necessity for scoops and towers to be orientated into the wind. A chimney is divided by partitions into four shafts, each open to a different direction, and regardless of the wind direction, one of the shafts will catch the breeze and the others will act as oast wind towers. This method was first adopted in Iran in the design known as the 'badgir' (see page 26).

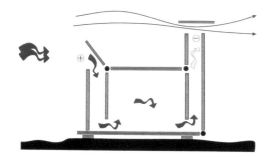

fig 26

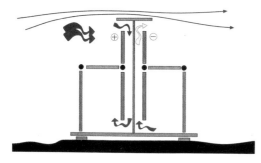

fig 27

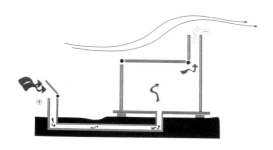

fig 28

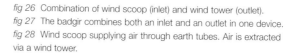

fig 26 Combination of wind scoop (inlet) and wind tower (outlet).
fig 27 The badgir combines both an inlet and an outlet in one device.
fig 28 Wind scoop supplying air through earth tubes. Air is extracted via a wind tower.

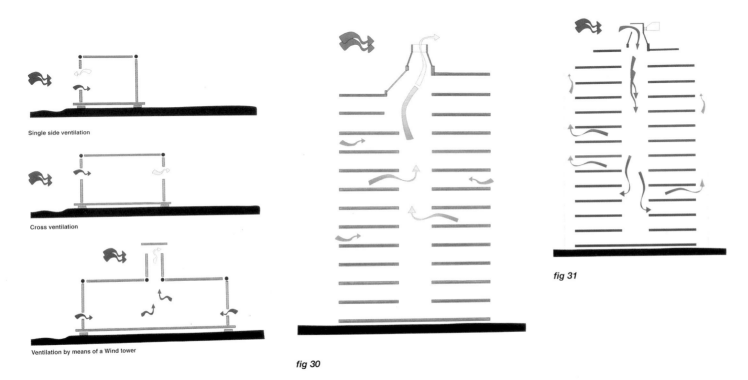

Single side ventilation

Cross ventilation

Ventilation by means of a Wind tower

fig 29

fig 30

fig 31

fig 29 Wind towers placed above a thermal flue to encourage stack effect and air movement.

fig 30 Wind towers placed above the atrium of a tower block to encourage air movement.

fig 31 Wind scoops placed at the top of a tower to 'catch' wind at high velocities and direct air into the building. Extract air can then be drawn out via thermal flues.

fig 32

PRECEDENT STUDIES

Before inventing or proposing new mechanical solutions, traditional solutions in vernacular architecture should be evaluated and then adopted or modified and developed to make them compatible with modern requirements… This process should be based on modern developments in the physical and human sciences, including the field of materials technology, physics, aerodynamics, thermodynamics, meteorology, and physiology.

Haasan Fathy

Before the industrial era, people in warm regions depended solely on natural sources of energy to ventilate and cool their houses. Systems and devices that harnessed the wind were therefore developed as a way of providing comfort within the building.

Towns and settlements originally established themselves upon hillsides and ridges in order to take advantage of the cooling effect of the increased wind speeds in these locations. As populations grew, people were forced to settle in harsher climates, and it is from the specific building forms and devices developed in these regions that most can be learnt about natural ventilation. These early examples of building ventilation may have been inspired by the natural world. Termites, for example, incorporate the basic principles of the stack ventilation system within their termitaries, which are often shaped for greater exposure along the east-west axis so that the vertical passages inside the mound will be warmed by the sun. Warm air will then rise up through the passages and in turn pull cooled air through the damp soil at the base of the mound. Wind passing over the mound also contributes to the chimney effect as negative pressure draws air up through the passages.

If we are to return to the use of natural energy solutions and move away from the unrestrained employment of mechanical ventilation of the late 20th century in order to conserve the planet's diminishing fuel resources and to protect our environment, it is necessary to carry out careful studies of traditional systems, such as the visually stunning examples of wind towers in the Middle East, North Africa and the Indian subcontinent (see below). An understanding of the complex relationship between buildings, microclimate and thermal comfort, along with an evaluation of building methods and materials, must be scientifically achieved. Modern engineering methods can then be applied to these systems to achieve a greater degree of accuracy and confidence.

fig 33

fig 32 *(opposite)* Wind towers, Yazd, Iran.
fig 33 Wind towers, Kerman, Iran.

HOT AND ARID ZONES

THE MALQAF

The malqaf (literally 'wind catcher') was used by the ancient Egyptians as early as 1300 BC and has long been a feature of the country's vernacular architecture.

The malqaf is a particularly suitable source of natural ventilation for buildings in hot, arid zones such as Egypt, where the use of large windows to provide adequate daylight has the drawback of letting in hot air and sand. The malqaf is a shaft that rises above the building and acts as a scoop to collect strong prevailing winds, channelling cool air through the building. In dense, urban environments this allows clean, strongly moving air to be collected away from street level. The air pressure outside is lower than the internal pressure, causing air to flow through the building.

The malqaf is fixed in place and carefully orientated at an angle to catch the prevailing winds, which may significantly alter in relation to the surrounding buildings, and indeed the building itself. The disadvantage of the malqaf is that, unable to rotate, it can only catch the prevailing wind. Its principle function, therefore, is as a climate modifier.

An excellent example of a malqaf is the Qa 'a of Muhib Ad-Dln Ash-Shaf 'l Al-Muwaqql in Cairo, which dates back to the 14th century. A large shaft rising high above the roof, it channels the cool breeze from the north into a central space. Air movement throughout the building is primarily caused by the pressure differential around the building. Outlets are provided via high-level storey windows above an open central space. Air movement by convection, produced by the stack effect, will also play its part when the external wind speed is low. The central space is surrounded by rooms that protect its sides from external heat, ensuring that a maximum temperature difference is achieved to encourage convection.

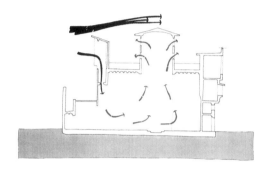

fig 34 The Qa 'a of Muhib Ad-Dln Ash-Shaf 'l Al-Muwaqql.

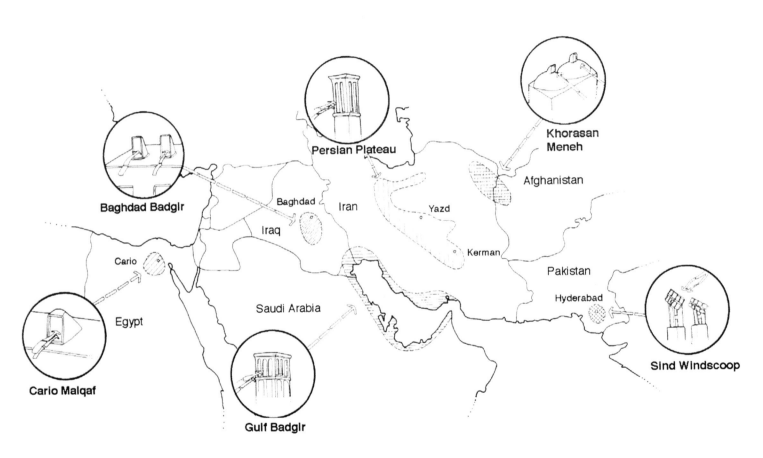

fig 35 Wind towers of the Middle East.

Baghdad Badgir

Cario Malqaf

Persian Plateau

Khorasan Meneh

Sind Windscoop

Gulf Badgir

Cario

Egypt

Baghdad

Iraq

Iran

Saudi Arabia

Yazd

Kerman

Afghanistan

Pakistan

Hyderabad

fig 36

THE BADGIR

The badgir (a refinement of the malqaf) was developed in Iran and other countries of the Gulf. It is a fixed device capable of acting as a wind scoop and exhaust. Its shaft is open at the top on four sides (occasionally only two), and a pair of partitions are placed diagonally across each other down its length. The wind towers are 3 by 3 metres and up to 7 metres high, with the upper section open to the wind in four directions. The badgir is able to catch breezes from any direction and channels a cool airflow into the room. It also acts as a chimney: hot air will be drawn through its leeward side due to the pressure difference over the chimney. When the winds are low, the towers continue to ventilate the rooms through stack effect alone.

Due to the wide-ranging temperature differences of the region, wind towers of the Arabian Gulf are unique. Summer temperatures may range from 32°C to 49°C at midday, but fall to 20°C or less at night, and in the winter the midday temperature range is between 20°C and 35°C, dropping down to 9°C at night. These extreme seasonal changes are reflected in the way the building is used. Badgirs are only effective at certain times of the day, and are more successful depending upon the season. Houses are therefore divided into two levels, the lower being occupied in the winter and the upper in the summer. The flat roof is also used for sleeping on summer nights. Three or more badgirs can often be seen on one building, providing ventilation to each of the summer bedrooms.

WIND SCOOPS

In the closely packed houses of Hyderabad in Pakistan, wind scoops have been in existence for at least 500 years. These are fixed in position to scoop up the prevailing afternoon winds, channelling cool air into each room of the multi-storey houses. Though these ingenious cooling devices are strikingly different in appearance from those found in the Arabian Gulf, they are an equally appropriate solution to the environmental problems of this region.

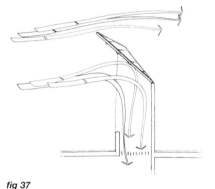

fig 37

fig 36 Badgir of Dubai, United Arab Emirates.
fig 37 Wind scoops, Hyderabad, Sind, Pakistan.

fig 38 Wind towers, Dubai, United Arab Emirates.

fig 39

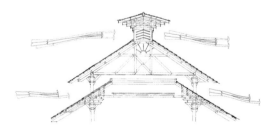

fig 40a

TROPICAL EXAMPLES

The humid climate of Malaysia averages air temperatures between 22°C and 32°C, with small annual and diurnal ranges. The winds blow in two dominant directions – from the northeast and southwest. On the equator, the wind is vertical and typically of low velocity. Windy days in Malaysia are as common as sunny days in the UK. To make use of the low power of the winds, the whole roof shape forms the wind tower and wind scoop.

The traditional Malaysian house is specifically designed to encourage ventilation by means of a number of devices. The building is raised on stilts to catch higher velocity winds, and cool air from the shady ground space is drawn up through the floorboards into the room above. As well as providing protection from the sun and rain, the high-pitched roof is constructed to provide ventilation of the roof space. A sail-like gable end directs air across the roof space to cool the house. Vents are built into the top of external walls to allow hot air to be drawn out into the roof space, from where it is then vented out. Air circulation through roof joints is also successful, ensuring effective ventilation of the roof and dissipating heat gain within it.

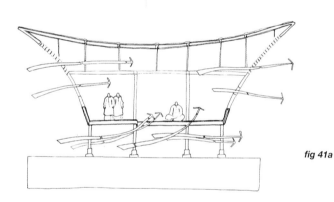

fig 41a

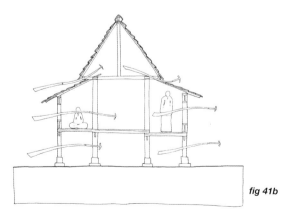

fig 40b

fig 39 Contemporary interpretation of the traditional Malay house by architect Jimmy Lim.
fig 40a, b Traditional Malay house. The roof provides ventilation for the building.
fig 41a, b Club Med resort based on a traditional Malay house by Hijjas Kasturi.

fig 41b

TEMPERATE EXAMPLES

The British Museum

The original British Museum Reading Room, built in 1857, provides an early example of wind-driven natural displacement ventilation. Its dome-shaped roof is vented at the top, and the negative pressure here will naturally draw the warm air out of the room. The negative displacement within the room will in turn draw air in from the courtyard to the basement, where it is distributed via underfloor vents. The thermal capacity of the walls in the basement enables the air either to be cooled or warmed, depending on the season, before entering the Reading Room.

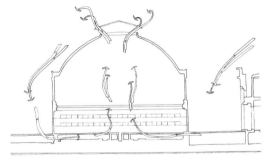

fig 42

Churches

Churches such as Putney Church in London have made use of their bell towers to provide effective ventilation. Air is brought into the building through equalising chambers to reduce the severity of draughts and currents; the foul exhaust air that collects at the roof is then drawn out through the tower. The bell tower incorporates ducts for airflow, which are acoustically separated from it.

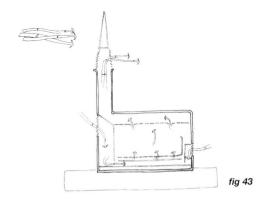

fig 43

Design for a theatre, 1872 – David Boswell Reid

Displacement ventilation through this theatre is achieved by the use of an omnidirectional cowl on the roof of the building, which can draw the extract air out, creating a displacement vacuum. Fresh air is then pulled in via a series of vents at high level, which ensures a continuous supply of clean air. The fresh air is taken down a shaft, where it can either be cooled in the summer by the use of fountains, or passed over heating coils in the winter, before emerging through underfloor vents. Valves are able to regulate the discharge of exhaust air as well as the ingress of fresh air.

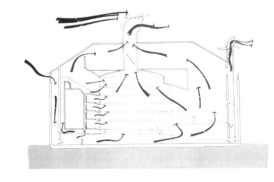

fig 44

fig 42 The British Museum Reading Room.
fig 43 The Bell Tower at Putney Church.
fig 44 Design for a theatre, 1872, by David Boswell Reid.

DESIGN OF WIND TOWERS AND WIND SCOOPS

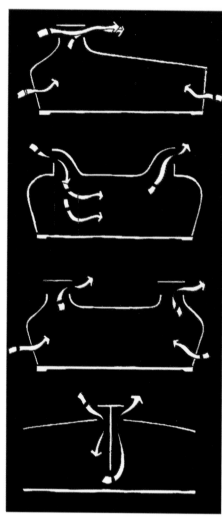

fig 45 From above: Wind tower; monodirectional wind tower and scoop; multidirectional wind tower and scoop; combined wind tower and scoop.

The design of wind towers and wind scoops is based on historical examples from the Middle East. These devices can be deployed to take advantage of particular site conditions, collecting cool winds, promoting cross-ventilation through the building and encouraging the extraction of excess warm air. Their application and design parameters will be studied to show how traditional devices can be adapted and improved in order to provide a simple and effective means of ventilation for even the most demanding buildings of the future.

WIND TOWERS

The effectiveness of wind towers is dependant upon producing the maximum pressure difference between the air inlet openings and the wind tower. The air movement around the building will determine the size and position of the wind tower and openings (and in some cases the actual building form), so as to maximise the pressure difference. The effects of resistance to the internal air movement can also dictate the internal layout.

Suitable building form

A pressure differential is created by a building in the path of an air stream. A positive pressure will be exerted on the windward face of the building, and a negative pressure will form over the roof and leeward face. The greater the restriction of air flow due to the building form (for example an elevation facing directly into the wind), the greater the positive pressure at the windward face. This will also produce a more powerful negative pressure over the roof and the wind tower. Additionally, the wind tower itself will act as an obstacle to the air flow, creating an area of positive pressure in front of the device, and a negative pressure over the opening of the chimney.

Alternatively, the building can be aerodynamically shaped to encourage an increased-velocity air stream over the building. This improves the 'draw' and therefore the performance of the wind tower.

The use of a wind tower allows the building to be orientated regardless of the wind direction. It can therefore point south to provide good solar access, even if the prevailing wind is from the east or west. This may not be possible with traditional cross-ventilation.

Optimum opening positions

The 'leading edge' of the building is the edge between the windward facade and the roof or sides. This is where the maximum positive pressure occurs – on the windward facade – and the maximum negative pressure occurs – on the roof (see figures 46 and 47).

A wind tower is at its most effective at the windward edge of the roof (where the negative pressure is greatest), and is least successful at the leeward edge. The ideal position, which can harness winds from all directions, is therefore at the centre of the building.

The position of the inlets is less crucial since it is the wind tower that will drive the air through the building. The ideal position for inlet openings is along the windward facade, where the positive pressure is at its greatest. However, the change of wind direction makes this difficult to obtain without a complex building-management system that can open and close windows/vents, and it is therefore better to have openings on all facades.

The positive pressure against the vertical facade increases with height. However, placing the openings at low level gets better results, allowing air flow to act in the same direction as internal stack effects and to circulate throughout the building.

Wind-tower height

The extrusion of a chimney produces the same effect as the building form by creating an obstacle and producing a negative pressure over the opening. The wind tower may be combined with the lift motor room, but it must be sufficiently high above the building to avoid any turbulence around the roof. Its height will also affect the ventilation rate: a taller tower will have stronger winds passing over it, creating a greater negative pressure. This must be weighed up against aesthetic concerns and planning restrictions.

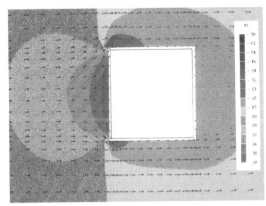

fig 46

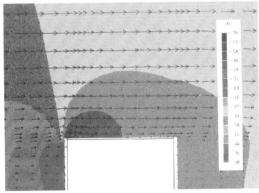

fig 47

fig 46 Plan – CFD analysis showing positive pressure on windward facade.
fig 47 Section – CFD analysis showing negative pressure over roof.

fig 48a

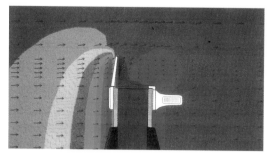

fig 48b

Design

The simplest design for a wind tower is a straight chimney, which will operate for all wind directions. A cover can be placed over the top, allowing wind to blow over the opening, but preventing rain from entering. In order to allow wind to blow freely between the top of the tower and the cover, the area of the gap in elevation should be greater than 40 per cent of the plan area of the tower.

A number of alterations can be made to the basic wind tower to increase the negative pressure at the opening. The exhaust air emitted from the chimney will interfere with the air stream passing immediately above the opening, and will disturb the air flow over the chimney, reducing the potential negative pressure. The following devices can be added to the chimney to allow the exhaust air to escape:

• *Oast wind towers* The overall performance of the oast wind tower will be nearly as effective as the chimeny, reducing the effect of interference from the exhaust air and the ingress of rain. However, it must be capable of orientating itself away from the wind.

• *Leading edge* Increasing the height of the chimney at the windward edge will allow the exhaust air to escape, at the same time maintaining a negative pressure over the opening. However, this requires the chimney, or a section of the chimney, to be omnidirectional.

• *Increasing the wind speed* Increasing the wind speed above the wind tower will produce a greater negative pressure over the opening. This can be done either by extending the height of the wind tower, or by developing an aerofoil wing.

The Venturi effect

Though there has been testing to produce a Venturi between the cover and the top of the tower to increase the suction within, this is not recommended. The system is based on the Bernoulli effect, which increases the air's velocity as it is forced through a reduced area. If the constriction between the wind tower and the Venturi cap is too small, the air will simply blow around the wind tower, rather than across the opening. The net result is a system less effective than a simple open-pipe chimney.

Sizing

The accurate sizing of wind towers to provide the required air-flow rate is described fully in *Wind Towers...* The size of opening depends on factors such as location, topography and shelter, as well as the required air-flow rate. As a rough guide, the total cross-sectional free area of the outlets should be no less than the following:

$$\frac{\text{total air volume (m}_3\text{/s)}}{1} = \text{m}^2 \text{ (free area)}$$

Other elements, such as the arrangement of the openings and any air flow resistance, will also determine the size and number of openings. The window openings for air intake should be at least twice the size of the wind tower to limit air-flow resistance. In winter, trickle ventilation should be catered for to ensure adequate air-change rates.

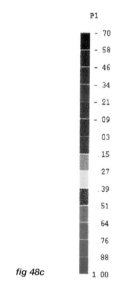

P1

- .70
- .58
- .46
- .34
- .21
- .09
  .03
  .15
  .27
  .39
  .51
  .64
  .76
  .88
  1.00

fig 48c

fig 48a, b, c CFD analysis showing the comparison of a straight pipe wind tower and a 'spade' wind tower with a windward leading edge.

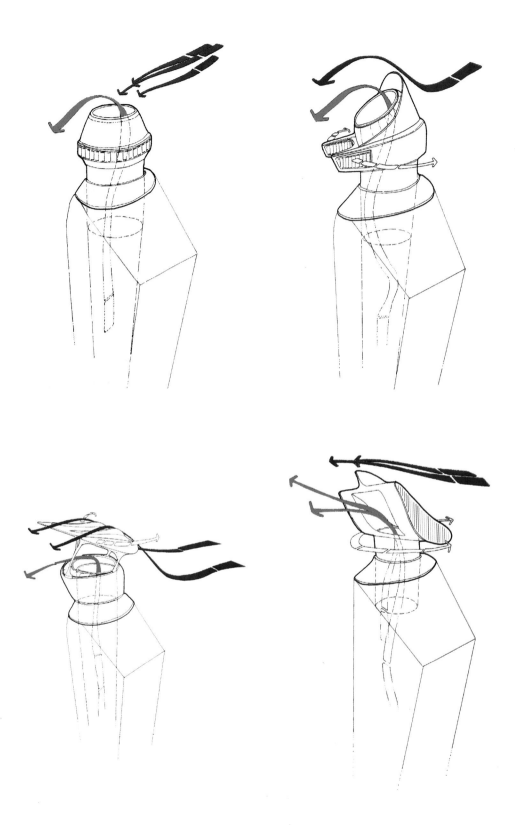

fig 49 Concept drawings for wind towers.

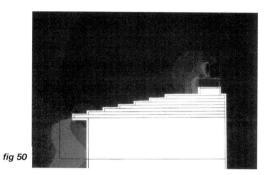

fig 50

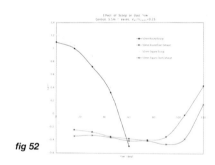

fig 51

fig 52

WIND SCOOPS

The effectiveness of a wind scoop is maximised by catching the wind at the area of greatest positive pressure and directing this air flow into the building. It should therefore be positioned clear of any building disturbances, for example, on the roof.

Suitable building form

If the form of the roof or the building directs the air stream up towards the scoop, the wind speed will be increased at the point of the scoop. This will augment the positive pressure against the wind scoop opening and enhance the effectiveness of the device.

Optimum opening positions

The greater the height above the roof, the more effective the wind scoop will be, due to the increased wind speed and reduced building interference. Although the roof of a building is under negative pressure, the presence of the wind scoop will provide an obstacle to the wind's air stream and therefore create a positive pressure against the scoop.

If the prevailing wind direction is not constant, the wind scoop will need to be omnidirectional and face into the wind in order to catch and direct the external air into the building. Extract air can then be removed through windows or vents along the leeward facade of the building, which is under negative pressure.

Alternatively, wind scoops can be placed in the ground, some distance from the building and the supply air can be brought in via earth tubes. Placed below the ground, these utilise the steady soil temperature to provide free cooling in peak summer and, conversely, warming in winter.

Design

The performance of wind scoops is dramatically reduced as the scoop deviates away from the head-on wind. At an angle of 30° yaw (deviation away from the head-on wind) the scoop starts to become ineffective; at 50° it is completely ineffective, and starts to act as an exhaust. The design of the scoop must therefore be very sensitive to wind direction changes and be capable of moving easily into the wind.

The opening for the wind scoop can be arc-shaped to help catch winds that deviate away from the head-on axis. The optimum arc angle is 90°, after which the wind starts to spill around the sides.

A balanced structure with a good centre of gravity is essential to allow the wind scoop to rotate easily. A single vane can be used to direct the scoop into the wind, although a double vane is more successful because it shortens the length of vane required.

fig 50 Section – CFD analysis showing the positive pressure at the scoop along the ridge of the roof. The design is considerably more effective from one direction and would only be used if there were a strong prevailing wind.

fig 51 A wind scoop is placed in the shaded landscape away from the building. The air is then supplied via earth tubes to the building. A wind tower is used for extraction.

fig 52 Graph showing the internal pressure measured against the yaw (deviation against the head-on wind measured in degrees). The oast exhaust is conventionally directed 180° away from the wind. The graph shows that the oast actually performs better as it deviates from the wind, and is most efficient at approximately 90°C. At this position, the negative pressure around the oast exhaust pipe is at its greatest. If the yaw is any greater than 90°, the oast begins to face into the wind and rapidly starts to lose efficiency.

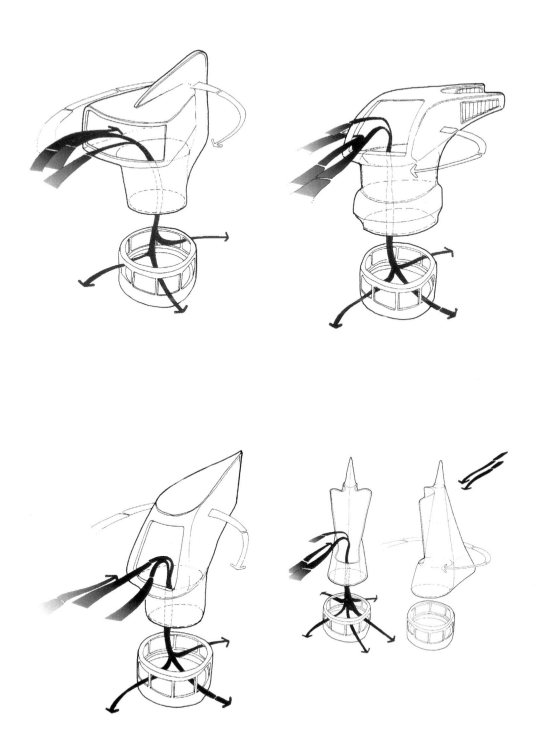

fig 53 Concept drawings for wind scoops.

WIND TOWERS OR WIND SCOOPS?

The type of building will often determine which particular form of wind-driven ventilation is most appropriate: wind towers, wind scoops, or a combination of both.

WIND TOWERS

The use of wind towers as a natural means of drawing air through the building has certain benefits and restrictions. The wind tower acts as an extract, and fresh air is supplied either through windows, vents, earth tubes or wind scoops. As with all wind-driven ventilation schemes, it is important to limit the resistance to air flow through the building. An open-floor plan is therefore generally required. Ventilation by means of wind towers can only provide a low-velocity air flow in comparison with mechanical ventilation. Ductwork must therefore be minimised, as grilles and junctions will reduce the air flow. The design of the building should encourage a natural air flow through the building towards the wind tower.

Open-plan offices

The use of wind towers to provide wind-driven ventilation is most suited to building types such as open-plan office buildings with an atrium or stair wells between the floors. Wind towers used in conjunction with atria have the primary advantage of being able to ventilate considerably more office area than standard cross-ventilation schemes, since all air movement will be towards the atrium. It is not uncommon for an atrium design to be incorporated within a modern office design to provide natural daylight.

Theatres and auditoriums

The large number of occupants within theatres and auditoriums creates high internal heat gains. This necessitates a system that provides a high air-change rate. The high internal heat will produce a stack effect, making a displacement ventilation system appropriate. Air can be supplied at low level and wind towers can remove the warm extract air collecting at the roof. Fresh air can be supplied either mechanically (mixed-mode) with extract through the wind tower, or via earth tubes.

This system of ventilation will be highly efficient, supplying clean air locally to the audience. Wind-driven natural ventilation is particularly advantageous for auditoriums since they are generally used during the evening when a lower external air temperature can be expected. However, there are a number of important design issues that must be addressed when naturally ventilating a theatre, such as the ingress of noise (see page 44). Careful detailing must ensure that attenuators and other fittings are designed to limit resistance to air flow.

Sports centres and terminals

Any large-volume space allows stratification to take place and therefore displacement ventilation by means of wind towers is effective. Open-plan building forms such as sports centres also present fewer problems of air flow restriction.

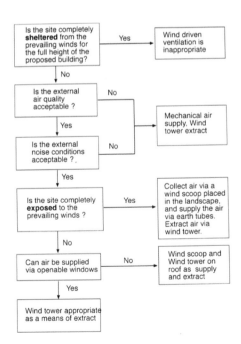

fig 54 Method of wind-driven ventilation appropriate for particular conditions.

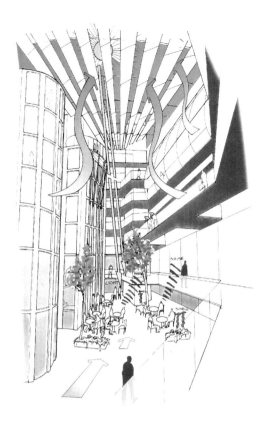

WIND SCOOPS

Wind scoops have very different characteristics from wind towers and are particularly effective in large-volume buildings, allowing the supply air to mix within the space. Because, in general, they supply air at a relatively high velocity, the point of supply into the space should not be immediately adjacent to the occupants.

Buildings in which the facade cannot be punctured for ventilation purposes because of site conditions such as noise infiltration, pollution and low air movement – often associated with urban environments – may utilise the wind scoop device. It may also be appropriate for an enclosed area of a building, such as an atrium. The atrium is naturally ventilated, while the surrounding building is mechanically air-conditioned.

Wind scoops can be placed on the roof of a building to catch the stronger, cleaner air at a higher elevation and redirect it into the building. A large volume will then allow the cool air to mix within the space. Alternatively, they can be placed in the ground, some distance away from the building. Supply air can then be brought into the building via earth tubes to provide low-level ventilation.

Atrium design

Atria often overheat due to a large area of exposed glazing. Placing wind scoops over the atrium can supply relatively large volumes by directing cool air in from above, which will drop into the space, mixing with and cooling the internal environment.

Shopping malls

Wind scoops act equally well for supplying air to shopping malls. The retail shops within the mall may have strict comfort criteria necessitating air-conditioning. However, the mall itself can be naturally ventilated to provide a clean, fresh environment, avoiding the often artificial atmosphere of the air-conditioned mall. A key design aim of shopping malls is to create the perception of being outside. Wind scoops provide the advantage of bringing the outside in, in terms of the combination of fresh air, light and external noise.

figs 55a, b Novello House. Architects: Whinney Mackay-Lewis Partnership. Structural and Environmental Engineers: Battle McCarthy.

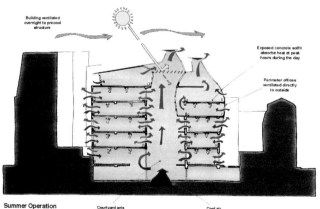

fig 55b

COMBINED WIND TOWERS AND WIND SCOOPS

One of the disadvantages of providing ventilation by means of the wind tower or the wind scoop is the issue of air movement through the facade. In the case of wind towers, the facade is used as a method of supply; in the case of wind scoops, as a method of extraction. A building with a wind tower must provide supply air through the windward facade to achieve maximum effect; the reverse is true of wind scoops, which are most successful when the air is exhausted at the leeward facade. This is problematic because the changes of wind direction (which alter the pressure coefficient of each particular facade), will affect the performance of the device. The only solutions are to have openable windows or vents on all facades, to design the system for 'worst-case scenario' wind direction, or to have an effective building management system that can open or close the appropriate apertures.

The combination of wind tower and wind scoop provides both supply and extract. The advantage of the combined system over the single device is that the air supply is collected at the roof. In urban conditions, the air will be stronger and cleaner at this level, and further removed from acoustic interference. Working together, the wind tower and scoop produce a greater pressure differential and consequently a more efficient system. This allows a reduction in the size of both the wind tower and scoop to provide adequate air flow.

Cellular offices

The increased pressure differential allows for a certain degree of ductwork between the wind tower/scoop and the area to be ventilated, which may not be possible with a single device. Natural ventilation can therefore be provided to cellular offices. Supply air is ducted from the scoop to underfloor vents, with extract air collected at ceiling height and directed to the wind tower. Additional resistance from fittings and ductwork should be accounted for when calculating the wind-tower or wind-scoop base area.

THE BADGIR

The badgir (see page 26) allows wind-driven ventilation to provide both air supply and extract without the expense and maintenance problems of an omnidirectional device. The angle of opening that can effectively catch the wind is 90°, which is the angle of each shaft. Tests also show that a wind tower is at its most effective at an angle of 90° away from the wind, where the maximum negative pressure occurs. The two shafts adjacent to that which catches the wind will therefore provide the most pressure difference to draw the extract air out of the building.

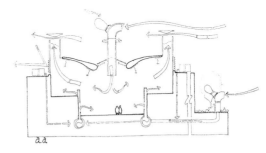

fig 56 A combination of wind towers and wind scoops used to ventilate a shopping centre.

MIXED-MODE APPROACH

The theory that a building must rely solely upon natural ventilation to be 'green', and that any use of mechanical systems compromises its integrity, is a misconception. For any number of reasons, a building may not be suitable for full natural ventilation. In these cases, natural systems can be combined with mechanical ventilation and/or air-conditioning in a mixed-mode approach that will produce considerable energy and cost savings.

Seasonal mixed-mode

If natural ventilation cannot ensure that an acceptable level of comfort is maintained throughout the year, a mixed-mode approach can be taken on a seasonal basis. Natural ventilation by means of either wind towers, wind scoops, or a combination of both, may be operated when external conditions permit (approximately 40 per cent of the time in the UK). Mechanical ventilation can be used when wind speeds are low or weather is extreme.

Zoning mixed-mode

A building can be zoned to facilitate natural ventilation in certain areas while others are air-conditioned. This principle caters for different uses within the same building. Atria, foyers and malls, for example, have less demanding criteria in terms of comfort than the restaurants, shops and offices they serve.

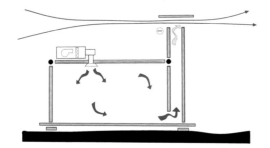

fig 57

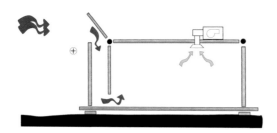

fig 58

fig 57 Air supplied mechanically, and extracted via the wind tower.
fig 58 Air supplied via wind scoop, and extracted mechanically.

APPLICATION

If the application of wind-driven ventilation is to be successful, there are certain fundamental issues that must be addressed, from the earliest concept stage through to detailed design. It is also important to understand the cost implications involved in the design and construction of a wind tower, so that an assessment of the overall budget can be compared against the reduction in plant size and reduced running costs. These issues include:

- site location and climatic restrictions
- building form and building fabric
- interaction with other building parameters
- flexibility
- cost-effectiveness
- user preferences.

Every building has its own particular parameters and it would be impossible to cover every application of wind-tower design here. Expert advice will therefore be necessary for some of the more complex design issues.

SITE LOCATION AND CLIMATIC RESTRICTIONS

Pollution and noise levels will influence the position of openings around the building, or if extreme, the feasibility of naturally ventilating a building. Natural ventilation in urban environments is therefore more challenging since these factors, plus reduced wind speeds, can restrict the use of ventilation at low level or through the facades. High-level ventilation via wind scoops may be necessary.

A particular site may be deemed too polluted, either now or in the future, to accommodate a building without filtration. A site with a high level of noise may also be inappropriate – the acoustic attenuation would be so great that a sufficient air flow would be unachievable. These factors must be carefully studied in advance.

Climatic restrictions

The success of the wind tower obviously depends on the wind speed of the area – coastal and open sites are subjected to higher wind speeds than sheltered or urban locations. The microclimate will also affect natural ventilation: it is important to study the site carefully. A wind break may shelter a site on which the wind tower, scoops or inlets are to be placed.

Heat gains

Care must be taken to control excessive heat gains. If these are extreme at certain times of the year then a mixed-mode system (combined mechanical and natural ventilation) may be preferable. Steps that minimise thermal loads, both climatically induced and internally generated, will reduce the required ventilation and consequently the wind tower size to a more manageable level.

BUILDING FORM AND BUILDING FABRIC

The form, layout and orientation of the building must be carefully thought out at the concept-design stage. The overall performance of the building fabric is also vital to ensure that solar gains are not excessive. Factors to be considered include:

• *Floor-to-ceiling height* Increasing the floor-to-ceiling heights and positioning air inlets at low level allows stratification to take place. The warm and polluted air will be lifted above the occupied zone due to stack effects, improving the quality of air within.

• *Plan width* The distance between the openings will affect the efficiency of the air flow and therefore the ventilation. This will depend on a number of factors, but as a general rule, for cross-ventilation this should not exceed five times the floor-to-ceiling height. The building-plan width may be twice this if a wind tower is centrally located.

• *Control* Minimising direct solar gain will reduce induced heat gains. However, this must be balanced against ensuring adequate daylight to prevent the use of artificial lighting. Some form of high-performance glazing and shading and the use of light shelves may be required. Orientation is another important factor to reduce the solar gain; the use of a wind tower allows a building to be orientated to provide solar access, rather than cross-ventilation determining the orientation.

• *Thermal capacity* The provision of thermal mass, such as exposed concrete ceilings, can prevent short-term fluctuations in heat gain and provide a degree of cooling if combined with night-time cooling.

• *Internal heat gains* Natural lighting levels should reduce the need for artificial lighting. Controls to switch off equipment when it is not in use are also important.

INTERACTION WITH OTHER BUILDING PARAMETERS

The application of wind towers and scoops may conflict with other building parameters. With an understanding of these oppositions, problems can be identified and resolved at an early stage. The main design parameters affecting wind-driven ventilation are:

• acoustic ingress and egress
• fire compartmentalisation
• security
• architecture
• controls
• weather proofing.

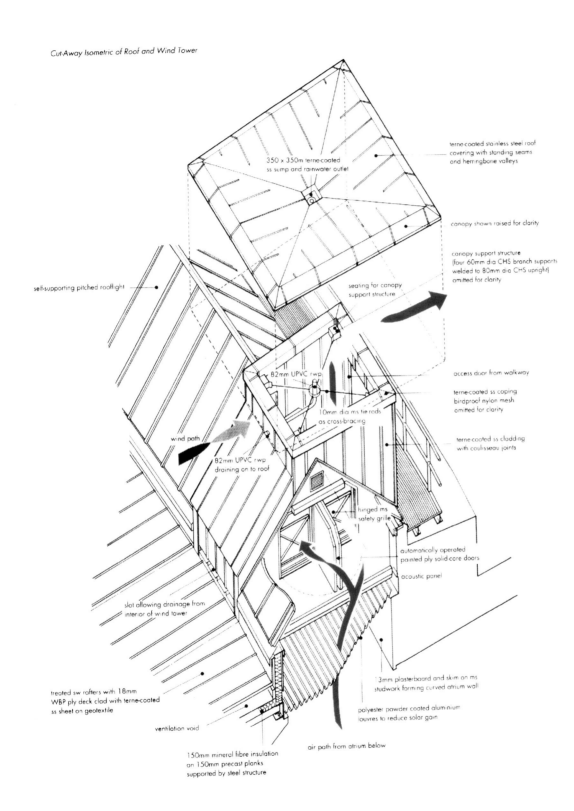

terne-coated stainless steel roof
covering with standing seams
and herringbone valleys

350 x 350m terne-coated
ss sump and rainwater outlet

canopy shown raised for clarity

canopy support structure
(four 60mm dia CHS branch supports
welded to 80mm dia CHS upright)
omitted for clarity

self-supporting pitched rooflight

seating for canopy
support structure

82mm UPVC rwp

access door from walkway

terne-coated ss coping
birdproof nylon mesh
omitted for clarity

10mm dia ms tie rods
as cross-bracing

wind path

terne-coated ss cladding
with coulisseau joints

82mm UPVC rwp
draining on to roof

hinged ms
safety grille

automatically operated
painted ply solid core doors

acoustic panel

slot allowing drainage from
interior of wind tower

13mm plasterboard and skim on ms
studwork forming curved atrium wall

treated sw rafters with 18mm
WBP ply deck clad with terne-coated
ss sheet on geotextile

polyester powder coated aluminium
louvres to reduce solar gain

ventilation void

air path from atrium below

150mm mineral fibre insulation
on 150mm precast planks
supported by steel structure

fig 59 Detail of wind tower (Ionica
Headquarters. Architects: RH Partnership,
Structural Specialists: Battle McCarthy.
See page 49).

Acoustic ingress and egress

Unlike mechanical ventilation, natural ventilation systems generate little noise. This is balanced against the fact that large external openings without acoustic attenuation will permit noise transfer between the building and outside. There is a fundamental design conflict between minimising the sound infiltration and the need to maximise air flow for naturally ventilated buildings. This is especially the case in urban environments.

Mechanically ventilated or air-conditioned buildings make use of high-velocity air movement through small-diameter ducting with appropriate acoustic attenuation to prevent noise infiltration. This is an energy-intensive system because duct fittings (including sound attenuation) with high resistance create a large pressure drop and therefore an increased power load is required.

The design of a naturally ventilated building cannot rely on a mechanically assisted pressure drop within the system. The introduction of flow resistance can critically affect the performance of the natural ventilation system. The use of long lengths of absorbent, lined ducting is therefore inappropriate and other systems must be adopted that can alleviate the problem of urban noise pollution without restricting the air flow. Three different acoustic strategies can be investigated:

- limited lined ductwork if the noise levels are low
- side-branch resonators to achieve low flow resistance and high acoustic attenuation
- electronic 'anti-noise' systems mounted within the ventilator–duct arrangement. (Active noise-control technology reads the soundwaves of the noise infiltration and produces a negative soundwave to eliminate it. This technology has been developed for the car industry and its utilisation for buildings is currently being researched. It offers the possibility of high noise attenuation, reduced air-flow resistance and low energy costs.)

It is likely that certain strategies will be more effective at low frequencies while others will succeed better at high frequencies. To achieve adequate acoustic performance over the audio frequency range encountered in urban noise a hybrid system will probably be the best solution. In all cases an experienced acoustic engineer should be consulted.

Fire compartmentalisation

For all buildings, smoke control must be considered at the earliest stages of the design. The principle behind wind towers is to extract air and therefore assist in providing smoke escape, but wind scoops need more careful consideration. During a fire, a wind scoop would need to be prevented from supplying air. One method would be to design the wind scoop to turn away from the wind in the case of a fire, and act instead as a wind tower, providing a smoke escape.

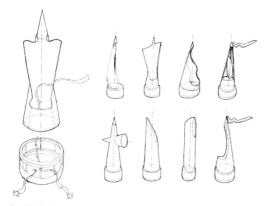

fig 60 Sculptural wind scoop.

The ability to ventilate naturally is reduced by floor-to-floor compartmentalisation due to the restriction of air movement. The compartmentalisation necessary to provide fire-escape routes must therefore be addressed.

An open-plan building will have fewer restrictions, but air flow through the building must be carefully designed. Air flow cannot be directed along fire corridors or fire escapes, which must be compartmentalised (this can sometimes be overcome with the use of electrical, self-closing fire doors). It may therefore be necessary to provide two routes to segregate the air-flow circulation and fire escape. This system of segregation incurs additional building costs and must be balanced against the savings made by eliminating the plant.

Security

In wind-driven, naturally ventilated buildings, openings are placed either within the facade or on the roof. These are often in the form of openable windows, which make the facade more vulnerable, and this can be a problem, particularly if the building is designed for night-time cooling.

To overcome these issues, the design of the windows, inlets and extracts must be carefully detailed. Vents, or small, high-level window openings offer better security.

Architecture

The inclusion of wind towers and scoops within a project can have a dramatic influence on the roofscape. Bold and expressive forms can enliven the roof-top, celebrating the building's low-energy virtues. This is not to say that the inclusion of a wind tower or wind scoop must necessarily become a feature of the building. The roof itself could be designed to act as a wind tower, providing wind-driven ventilation without the extrusion of an actual tower.

Controls

The ventilation and air-change rate will be determined by controlling the amount of air that passes through the openings. Extract air drawn through the wind tower can be controlled with a series of adjustable dampers, and air intake can be manipulated with openable windows or vents. It is important to ensure that the size of the openings can be adjusted to serve the different conditions such as summer/winter and day-time/night-time cooling. One solution is to specify low-level, manually openable windows for summer conditions, and high-level, mechanically operated windows or vents for winter ventilation and night-time cooling. Night-time cooling requires fewer air changes and a smaller area of opening provides better security.

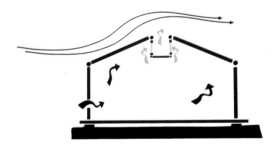

fig 61 Wind tower built into the roof.

Weather proofing

The inclusion of wind towers and wind scoops within a project effectively creates large openings in the roof. The wind tower or scoop must therefore be designed to prevent the ingress of rain. Weather proofing can be dealt with in a number of ways, depending on the device used.

The obvious solution is a cap, allowing the wind to flow over the opening while providing protection from the rain. But because the height between the top of the chimney and the cap is crucial, this must be carefully tested. If the cap is too close to the opening, the air flow across the chimney will be restricted and the performance reduced. In general, a cap should be positioned above the chimney at a distance of half the diameter. The cap, however, will only prevent the ingress of vertical rain; wind-driven rain must also be dealt with. Placing louvres between the cap and the pipe will prevent rain from entering but will seriously reduce the air flow across the pipe and is therefore not recommended. If louvres are used, this must be taken into account when sizing the wind tower. An alternative method of dealing with rain is to place a tray within the pipe. The water can then be collected within the chimney and drained off.

Oast chimneys offer more protection from the rain, and if omnidirectional they will turn their backs on the wind-driven rain. The reverse is true in the case of wind scoops.

FLEXIBILITY

To ensure that a structure has a long life, it must be designed to be flexible. Buildings should encompass alteration at all levels, including open-plan to cellularisation, or change of use. In order to provide a truly flexible building, the design should allow for the incorporation of a cooling system. Contingency planning to provide sufficient plant-room space and duct risers can be provided, as well as adequate floor-to-ceiling height for potential ductwork.

Robustness

A well-designed naturally ventilated building is less likely to undergo failure modes, due to the reduction in the number of components susceptible to malfunction. The life of a mechanical plant is usually about half that of the building, and there are therefore significant cost implications in eliminating mechanical ventilation.

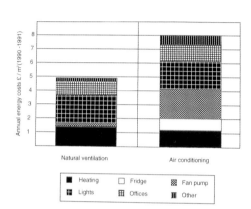

fig 62

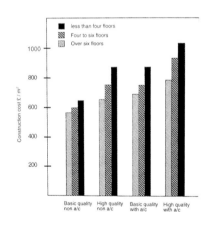

fig 63

fig 62 Energy costs for naturally ventilated open-plan and air-conditioned buildings.

fig 63 Cost comparison for air-conditioned and naturally ventilated speculative buildings by Gardiner & Theobald. These figures are indicative only and a specific analysis should be carried out for each project.

COST-EFFECTIVENESS

Capital costs

The elimination of plant reduces capital costs with respect to HVAC systems. However, cost comparisons should be carried out over the whole building. Wind-driven ventilation may have hidden budgetary implications. The required air-flow rate may only be achievable with the addition of a number of other elements such as:

• improving external shading to prevent solar gain

• increasing structural mass to provide thermal mass (this may require extra groundwork)

• providing more openable windows.

A specific analysis should therefore be carried out for each project to give an accurate cost comparison.

Space savings

A naturally ventilated building will require less space for plant rooms and service distribution ducts, but other factors must also be considered:

• greater floor-to-ceiling heights may be required to allow for displacement ventilation

• circulation areas may need to be increased to allow for adequate air movement.

Operating costs

Naturally ventilated buildings can reduce or eliminate the need for fans and chillers, which are usually electrically powered, and therefore reduce the operating costs of a building. According to a survey of 1993, the energy costs of air-conditioned buildings are 40 per cent more than non air-conditioned buildings.

Maintenance costs

A further survey undertaken by chartered surveyor and letting agent Jones Lang Wootton in the mid-90s, found that naturally ventilated buildings paid service charges of approximately £3 per square metre compared with air-conditioning of more than £12 per square metre. The greater the simplicity of the design, the lower the maintenance costs for the building. However, wind-driven ventilation requires special maintenance factors including:

• variable grilles and dampers to control air flow

• movable elements such as wind scoops.

Other factors like cleaning costs, which may be higher due to the unfiltered air being used, should also be taken into account.

USER PREFERENCES

A recent study of 480 offices by the chartered surveyors Richard Ellis found that 89 per cent of occupants preferred buildings that were not air-conditioned, the most important factors being the provision of good daylight and ventilation via openable windows.

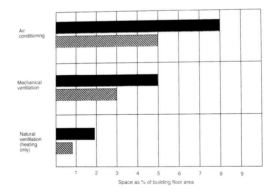

fig 64 Space requirements of HVAC systems as a percentage of gross building area for different ventilation strategies.

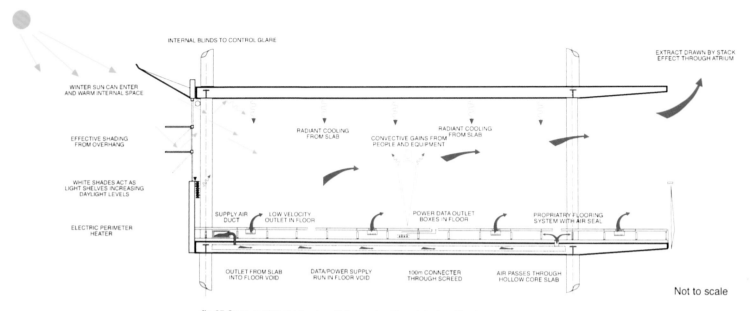

INTERNAL BLINDS TO CONTROL GLARE

EXTRACT DRAWN BY STACK
EFFECT THROUGH ATRIUM

WINTER SUN CAN ENTER
AND WARM INTERNAL SPACE

EFFECTIVE SHADING
FROM OVERHANG

RADIANT COOLING
FROM SLAB

RADIANT COOLING
FROM SLAB

CONVECTIVE GAINS FROM
PEOPLE AND EQUIPMENT

WHITE SHADES ACT AS
LIGHT SHELVES INCREASING
DAYLIGHT LEVELS

ELECTRIC PERIMETER
HEATER

SUPPLY AIR
DUCT

LOW VELOCITY
OUTLET IN FLOOR

POWER DATA OUTLET
BOXES IN FLOOR

PROPRIATRY FLOORING
SYSTEM WITH AIR SEAL

OUTLET FROM SLAB
INTO FLOOR VOID

DATA/POWER SUPPLY
RUN IN FLOOR VOID

100m CONNECTER
THROUGH SCREED

AIR PASSES THROUGH
HOLLOW CORE SLAB

Not to scale

fig 65 Cross section of natural ventilation system through Ionica office floor.

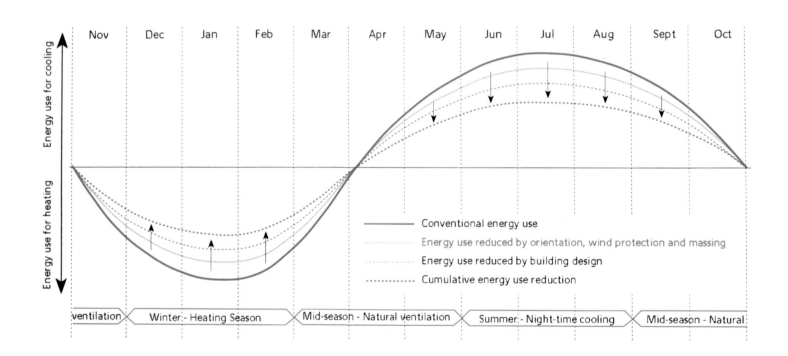

fig 66 Energy consumption and reduction by means of building design, orientation, wind protection and massing.

IONICA HEADQUARTERS

Cambridge, UK

The Ionica Telecommunications headquarters is a good example of a building with high internal gains that can provide comfortable conditions by means of natural ventilation. An enlightened brief called for an energy-efficient building that allowed the option of opening windows, rather than the traditional, hermetically sealed, air-conditioned box. Battle McCarthy's approach, working with the RH Partnership, was to devise a building strategy that would allow the building to operate with the minimum of mechanical equipment and, therefore, energy consumption.

Design objectives were to produce a daylit, naturally ventilated building with a high-quality working environment. A central atrium is the standard device to allow daylight penetration into a deep-plan office as well as providing good natural cross-ventilation. The innovative design principle behind the Ionica Headquarters was to place wind towers along the top of the atrium, allowing cross-ventilation to be driven through the building in a controllable manner, even during high winds.

The Ionica Headquarters is designed to utilise the pressure differential surrounding the building. Fresh air will enter through the facades under positive pressure. The wind towers positioned on the roof are under negative pressure for all wind directions. This pressure difference ensures an air flow from the offices to the atrium and out of the building. If the wind velocity drops below a certain level (1–2.5m/s) then buoyancy-driven flow can be relied upon. Warm air will naturally rise through the building and out through the wind towers. To further encourage the stack effect, a glazed atrium is positioned below the wind towers, which encourages heat to build up along the roof. Fixed louvres below the sunspace prevent solar radiation from penetrating the interior.

The wind towers were designed to draw air through the building regardless of the external wind direction. Wind-tunnel testing was used extensively to determine air movement through particular building forms at an early stage of the process, significantly changing the design of the tower.

Initially, the wind tower had louvred openings on four sides, but this did not produce an efficient system. Testing showed that in certain conditions the louvred wind tower actually produced a positive downflow into the building. The solution was to create an 'open-top chimney' with a cap and floor to prevent rain ingress. Air is drawn in via controllable doors on each side of the tower, which then acts like a 'plenum'. These doors also control the flow of air through the building. As the wind speed increases, so the suction increases. The air flow can be reduced from 100 per cent to 15 per cent by gradually closing the doors.

Another design factor that was critical to the success of the ventilation system was the position of the wind towers. The building is oriented on an east-west axis and therefore, if the wind were blowing from the east or west along the length of the building, curvature would ensure that one wind tower would not 'shadow' the next.

Four distinct seasonal conditions were studied, with both day- and night-time modes. To guarantee comfort in extreme climatic conditions the building was designed with a mixed-mode approach to ventilation. It is ventilated naturally for the majority of the year, but mechanically if heat gain or loss is too great. A comprehensive building management system is therefore crucial for a structure of this nature. An intelligent control system is able to monitor weather changes and control the operation of both the passive and active environmental systems to ensure the most efficient use of energy. This provides the ability to learn how the building responds to various weather changes and to adjust the systems accordingly.

Energy use for the natural ventilation strategy, using good external shading, exposed thermal mass and wind towers, was predicted at 130 kWh/m2/year. This shows a 46 per cent saving on a good-quality, air-conditioned building.

SUMMARY DATA
Client
St John's College
User
Ionica Telecommunications
Location
St John's Innovation Park, Cambridge, UK
Architect
RH Partnership
Environmental & Structural Specialists
Battle McCarthy
Building Services Engineer
Ribka Battle
Structural Engineer
Hannah, Reed and Associates
Quantity Surveyor
Davis Langdon and Everest

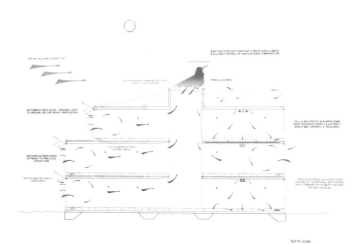

fig 67a Mid-season day-time operation.

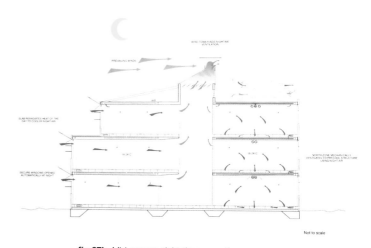

fig 67b Mid-season night-time operation.

fig 68 Exterior.

fig 69 Full-scale mock-up of Bluewater Shopping Centre wind scoop for performance monitoring.

BLUEWATER SHOPPING CENTRE

Dartford, Kent, UK

Traditionally, the shopping mall has been an artificially lit, air-conditioned space. Rather than creating a protected environment, the 'internal street' has induced feelings of enclosure, lethargy and even Sick Building Syndrome. Eric Kuhne Associates, with Battle McCarthy Consultant Engineers, set about designing a 'shopping avenue' that possesses all the benefits of an outdoor street, such as sunshine and a fresh breeze, but filters out the unpleasant aspects such as noise and pollution.

The key to the success of this approach is to eliminate the standard air-conditioned mall solution and develop a natural ventilation system that will introduce a fresh natural breeze along the concourse. This not only provides cost and environmental advantages but is also physiologically beneficial, avoiding the sense of enclosure of a sealed, environmentally air-conditioned box. Good air supply within a mall should have a variety of speeds so that the user may find his or her own particular comfort range. Natural ventilation can provide this whilst creating a sense of external conditions. It also establishes a sound environmental policy by reducing carbon dioxide emissions.

Wind scoops are particularly effective when supplying large open spaces such as atria because air does not have to be supplied adjacent to the occupants. Fresh air is introduced to Bluewater shopping centre by a series of 2-metre-high conical wind scoops, which owe their form to the influence of traditional Kent oast houses (acting as wind towers). These are mounted on the roof to allow cooler air to drop and mix within the space. Placed at 15-metre intervals along the centre line of the mall, they catch the external air stream and provide fresh air to the building.

The scoops were designed to rotate on a vertical axis into the wind, ensuring continuous air supply regardless of wind direction. The rotating scoop is guided by two parallel wind vanes, which were found to be more stable than a single central vane. In the event of a fire, the vanes can be released so that the scoop is rotated away from the wind and acts as a wind tower, extracting smoke from the mall.

To ensure the quality of fresh air, monitoring for pollutants is of great importance. This information can be used to control air-intake rates, the location of air intake, temperature and humidity in the mall.

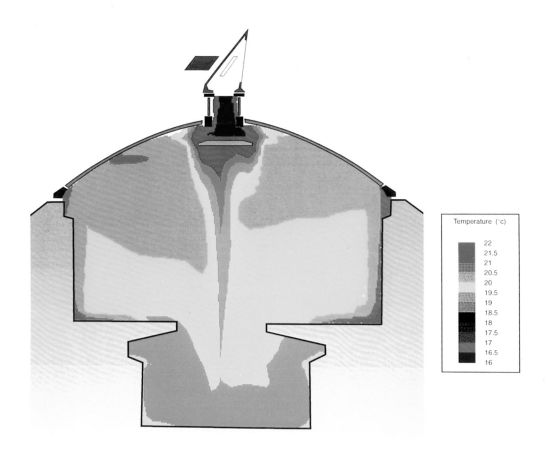

Temperature (°c)

22
21.5
21
20.5
20
19.5
19
18.5
18
17.5
17
16.5
16

fig 70a

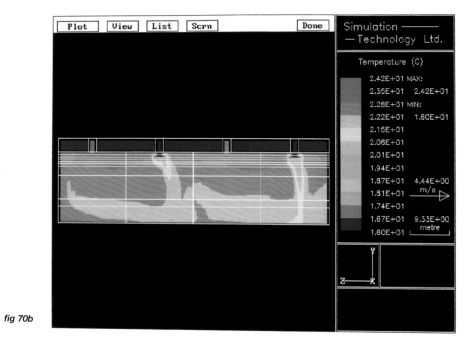

| Plot | View | List | Scrn | | Done |

Simulation ——— —Technology Ltd.

Temperature (C)

2.42E+01 MAX:
2.35E+01   2.42E+01
2.28E+01 MIN:
2.22E+01   1.60E+01
2.15E+01
2.08E+01
2.01E+01
1.94E+01
1.87E+01   4.44E+00
1.81E+01   m/s
1.74E+01
1.67E+01   9.33E+00
1.60E+01   metre

fig 70b

figs 70a b CFD analysis showing cool air supplied via wind scoops on the roof, and air movement within the shopping mall.

SUMMARY DATA

Client

Land lease

Location

Bluewater, Dartford, Kent, UK

Architect

Eric Kuhne Associates: Benoys

Environmental & Structural Specialists

Battle McCarthy

Building Services Engineer

Roberts and Partners

Structural Engineer

Watermans

Quantity Surveyor

Cyril Sweets

figs 71a b The wind scoops create an architectural feature of the roof.

fig 71a

fig 71b

fig 72 Architectural model.

SUMMARY DATA

Client

Lion of Kenya Insurance Company

Location

Nairobi, Kenya

Architect

Planning System Services

NAIROBI TOWER

Kenya

The client required a new office building that would necessitate minimum energy expenditure in the provision of acceptable thermal conditions for its occupants. The proposed site is in the elevated outskirts of Nairobi, Kenya.

The design team interpreted the brief as an opportunity to utilise passive conditioning of the internal environment. The first step was to gain an understanding of the local weather. Major characteristics are the predominance of north-easterly winds, the lower-than-expected peak ambient air temperature of 28°C, a narrow diurnal temperature range and high global solar radiation.

The design seeks to capitalise on the opportunity for controllable natural ventilation presented by the largely uniform wind direction, whilst attempting to minimise the potential for excessive solar gains.

The central strategy for internal thermal conditioning is, therefore, natural ventilation. The design allows air into the building at both high and low level, pulling it though the occupied spaces by maintaining a positive pressure difference between the points of air inlet and exhaust.

The office accommodation will be arranged over 18 floors, built above four floors of trading premises. Two shafts run continuously from the lowest office floor to the roof, where they connect to a single wind scoop, oriented to capture the north-easterly winds. At low level they are open to a 'dummy' floor. Louvred openings connect the shafts to each floor, allowing occupants to regulate air flow onto the floor in response to the conditions experienced, whilst a rooftop weather station regulates flow into the two shafts in relation to the ambient conditions.

The natural ventilation provides both fresh air and the means of heat dissipation. It is likely that the latter will predominantly determine the necessary ventilation rate. To be successful, a natural ventilation strategy must be accompanied by measures to minimise heat gains to the space. Whilst internal gains from lights and machines can be minimised by careful specification and control strategies, without suitable design provision the major heat gain to the offices would be solar. To prevent excessive solar gain, the building includes a double-skin facade. This consists of a weatherproof inner leaf, clear single glazing, plus a second skin cantilevered from the building perimeter. The flue thus created will be utilised as the office-exhaust air path, whilst simultaneously removing solar heat conducted through the glazing. The flue extends the full height of the building, terminating above roof level.

Whilst all the necessary solar control could be provided by solar-control glazing in the outer leaf, the corresponding reduction in light transmission would probably necessitate the continuous use of artificial lighting, thereby replacing one heat gain with another. Therefore, the control of solar gains will be shared between the outer leaf and an

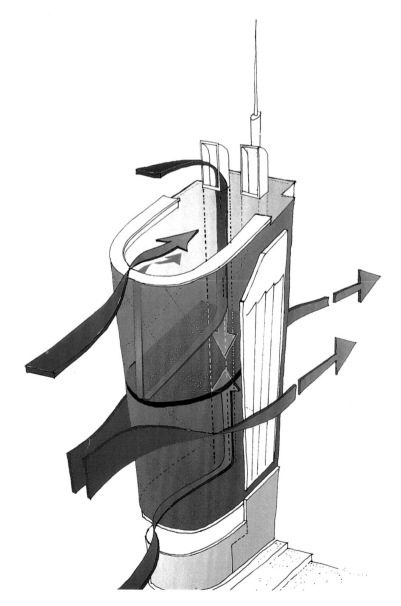

fig 73 Outline of natural ventilation strategy.

occupant-controlled retractable blind, positioned in the flue. Thermal analysis was used to determine the optimum balance between solar control and provision of daylight for the facade. This concluded that there was a need for high-solar-absorbing glass, with a fritting applied to the sections above and below the viewing panel. For reasons of practicality, the blind was positioned adjacent to the inner leaf, although the optimum position would otherwise be adjacent to the outer leaf.

Within the offices, the concrete ceiling soffits will be exposed. Due to its high thermal capacity, the concrete will have a surface temperature lower than that of the air. This will benefit occupant comfort in two ways: firstly as a heat sink, and secondly by reducing the resultant temperature at a given air temperature. It is the resultant temperature that should be used to measure the thermal conditions as perceived by occupants. If the heat-sink capacity is not to be gradually reduced, it is important that the heat absorbed by the structure is removed overnight. However, natural night cooling may be insufficient due to the narrow diurnal temperature range. Therefore, provision has been made for the inclusion of mechanical plant for forced night cooling.

Computer simulation was used extensively during the design process. Dynamic thermal analysis enabled prediction of resultant temperatures within the occupied spaces for building models with different facades, internal finishes and ventilation openings. Features integral to the natural-ventilation strategy were optimised using Computational Fluid Dynamics (CFD). These studies centred on the inlets and outlets. The flow into the building via the wind scoop was shown to increase when the internal profile was curved. Flow at the top of the building was studied to ensure that openings from the top of the double-skin facade were positioned in a region of negative pressure. Within the 'dummy' floor guide, fins will be positioned to obstruct flow across the space, directing air towards the base of the shafts. CFD was used to determine the position and shape of these guide fins, which removed the need for mechanically controlled shutters.

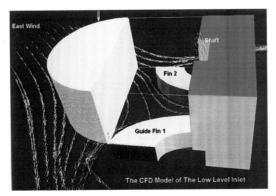

fig 74 CFD image showing flow across dummy floor to ventilation shaft.

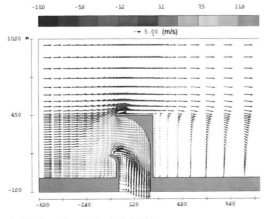

fig 75 Flow into optimised wind scoop.

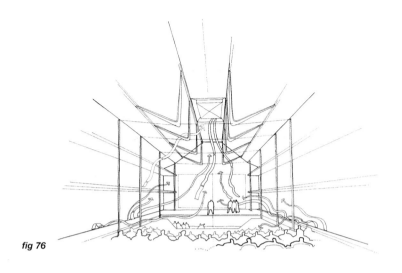

fig 76

figs 76-77 Computational Fluid
Dynamic Analysis of the air
movement from the floor grilles to
the wind tower of Gresham School
Theatre.
fig 78 Air movement through the
building supplied via earth tubes at
ground level and exiting via wind
towers.

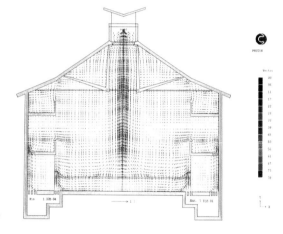

fig 77

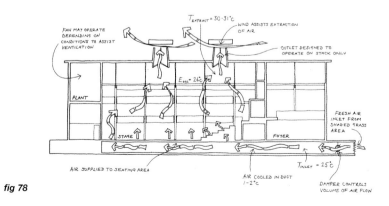

fig 78

GRESHAM SCHOOL THEATRE

Norfolk, UK

Ventilating an auditorium without mechanical assistance is problematic due to the large air-change rates required and the heat gains from occupancy, equipment and lighting. The principle behind the natural ventilation of Gresham School Theatre is to create negative displacement ventilation, generated by two wind towers placed on the roof. Wind passing across the towers creates a negative external pressure. Along with stack effects occurring due to internal gains, this will then draw air out of the auditorium. The exiting warm air creates a negative displacement, which will in turn draw fresh air into the auditorium through inlet ducts under the seating and the floor.

Air is pulled into the theatre via two underground earth tubes, which are situated on either side of the auditorium. This system of supply has a number of benefits due to the high heat storage properties of soil. In the summer, the earth temperature is lower than the external air temperature, so air passing underground, combined with the cooler surface of the concrete ducts, produces a form of free cooling. Conversely, the chill will be removed from winter air by the relatively warm surface of the duct.

The earth tubes are designed to incorporate acoustic attenuation in the form of attenuation splitters, but these had to be carefully detailed to minimise the resistance of the air flow through the duct. A vermin screen is also fitted, along with motorised dampers that connect to a building-management system to provide the necessary control of ventilation. The earth tubes also have the advantage of removing the ventilation ductwork from the occupied areas.

SUMMARY DATA

Client
Gresham School Theatre General Charitable Trust
User
Gresham School Theatre
Location
Norfolk, UK
Architect
RHWL Architects

Environmental Engineer
Battle McCarthy
Structural Engineer
Battle McCarthy
Acoustic Engineer
Arup Associates
Quantity Surveyor
Baker Mallet

fig 79 Skyline view of Queens Building.

QUEENS BUILDING, DE MONTFORT UNIVERSITY

Leicester, UK

The Queens Building uses two-thirds of the energy of a typical, well-designed, naturally ventilated building and half that of a similar air-conditioned structure. It provides teaching, laboratory and research facilities, whilst also acting as an object for study. Its services are deliberately exposed. Maximum use is made of daylight, which greatly reduces running costs.

The unconventional structure dissolves considerable volumes into narrow section elements, with free elevations on three sides. Sunlight penetrates the laboratory and concourse areas deep in the core of the building through extensive windows and glazed gables, which also supply ample light to the drawing studios. Supplementary artificial lighting and carbon-dioxide emissions are significantly reduced.

In the summer, the building is cooled by cross-ventilation where the section is narrow. In deep plan areas, such as the mechanical laboratory, purpose-made ventilation openings and honey-combed brickwork allow air into the seven buttresses supporting the external wall and gantry crane track. Roof vents in the laboratory open automatically to create a draught. Low-level air inlets and stacks induce air flow in the auditorium.

Air enters at the street side of the auditorium through a large opening, protected from the weather. It passes through motorised volume-control dampers at the building envelope line, then through an acoustically lined plenum, and is distributed through the void under the seating. It subsequently passes over finned heating tubes suspended under the seats, then through a grille of aluminium mesh. There are no air filters, which would create too high a resistance to air flow.

The air heated by occupants and other internal elements such as lighting and audio-visual equipment rises through the auditorium into the diamond-shaped exhaust stacks, which also serve as supports for the drawing-studio roof trusses. The total cross-section free area of the two stacks is 3 square metres. Above the stacks are automatically controlled opening windows with a total free area of approximately 7.9 square metres. The opening area is based on a rule of thumb for chimney tops: the area of the vertical opening faces should be at least twice the flue cross-sectional area. The discharge coefficient for windows varies from approximately 0.57 at an opening of 60° to 0.63 at 90°. A slight overhang at the top of the stacks helps prevent rain from entering.

Key points in the design of the auditorium are:
• The spaces have high thermal mass and high ceilings. In summer the building is pre-cooled at night by allowing air movement through the room. This helps to lower daytime temperatures.
• The air path is mainly unrestricted.
• The stacks terminate approximately 3 metres above the roof line to avoid local turbulence. Air exhausts exit via automatic opening windows at the stack tops.

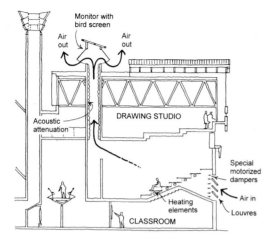

fig 80 Air passage through auditorium.

Labels in figure: Monitor with bird screen; Air out; Air out; Acoustic attenuation; DRAWING STUDIO; Special motorized dampers; Air in; Heating elements; Louvres; CLASSROOM

Performance

The building, and in particular the auditorium, has been extensively studied and monitored. Noise levels have been found to be acceptable, and temperatures in the auditorium remain comfortable at 20 to 24°C, even when the external temperature rises above 30°C. During the very hot summer of 1995, of all of De Montfort's 250,000 square metres of building stock, the chief engineer stated that his first choice for refuge from the heat was the Queens Building.

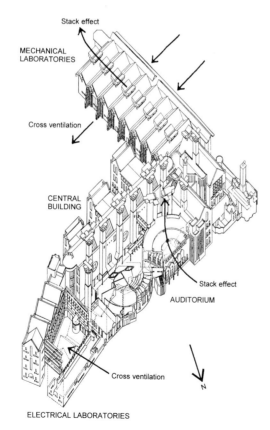

DE MONTFORT UNIVERSITY

Labels in figure: Stack effect; MECHANICAL LABORATORIES; Cross ventilation; CENTRAL BUILDING; Stack effect; AUDITORIUM; Cross ventilation; N; ELECTRICAL LABORATORIES

fig 81 Axonometric of Queens Building.

SUMMARY DATA

Client
De Montfort University

Location
Leicester, UK

Architect
Short Ford and Associates

Services Engineer
Max Fordham Associates

Structural Engineer
YRM/Anthony Hunt Associates

Quantity Surveyor
Dearle and Henderson, London

Landscape Architect
Livingston Eyre Associates

Main Contractor
Laing Midlands

Mechanical Contractor
How Engineering

Electrical Contractor
Hall and Stinson

fig 82 Interior of auditorium.

ECOTOWER

Kowloon, Hong Kong

The EcoTower is a proposal, developed with Terry Farrell and Company, for a tower appropriate for the tropics, based on four fundamental engineering design principles:

- structural behaviour
- ventilation, temperature and humidity control
- solar and daylight control
- power supply and service.

The tower is 1 kilometre high, on a 100-metre diameter base plate, providing 900,000 square metres of office and residential accommodation. An equivalent conventional office development in the tropics would have a total energy demand of about 650 kwh/m2 and would generate annual carbon dioxide emissions equivalent to the weight of 2.5 million people. The EcoTower proposal grew out of the desire to reduce the energy consumption to less than a third. This would be achieved by minimising carbon dioxide emissions, and by creating an energy strategy that exploits ambient renewable energies and changes in environmental conditions throughout the building's height. In Hong Kong, for example, although the humidity remains constant with height, the air temperature drops 1°C per 100 metres and the wind is stronger and more predictable with altitude.

Rather than engineering an altered and controlled environment within each of the blocks separately, the EcoTower creates one large, enclosed space, the environment of which may be controlled more efficiently using 'broad brush' techniques. The radial arrangement of building blocks creates a structure with a maximum number of facades that are shaded from direct sun at any time. The scale of the proposal and the active facade system, which is wrapped around the blocks to form a cylindrical enclosure, create a controlled 'external' environment for the building using ambient energy sources such as wind and solar radiation. This active facade controls the quantity of light and heat energy allowed into the development and, with the perimeter cores, absorbs energy via photovoltaics. Dramatic variations in climatic conditions over its height – including a 10°C temperature variation – enable the building to produce a stack effect, which allows cross-ventilation of the blocks. Wind turbines, mounted on the building, take advantage of the near-constant winds at high altitudes.

Structure

The tower consists of 40 storey units suspended from transfer structures, which span between the perimeter cores, founded upon a basement raft on suitable bearing strata. The positioning of these cores at the edge of the envelope creates lateral stability with the minimum amount of structure, shades the buildings from the sun, and provides an ideal surface for the positioning of photovoltaics.

Ventilation, thermal and humidity control strategy

The artificial environment created within the building envelope is suitable for openable windows, allowing natural ventilation all year round.

As the air temperature at the top of the tower is 10°C lower, it is cooled further, dehumidified and then allowed to free-fall down the central well. The result is that the warmer air at the perimeter rises to the top – in a conventional stack effect – drawing exhaust air from the offices and creating a passive air cycle, the 'coolth' from the passing air cooling the incoming fresh air. In addition, rain and condensed vapour is collected and allowed to flow down the outer face of the cores. As the wind passes them, evaporation occurs, reducing their temperature.

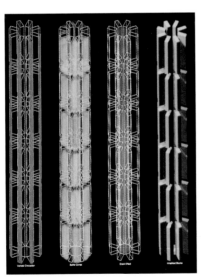

fig 83

SUMMARY DATA
Location
Kowloon, Hong Kong
Architect
Terry Farrell and Partners
Environmental Engineer
Battle McCarthy

Intelligent skin

The skin of the outer envelope will respond to changing conditions, excluding solar energy when necessary. To accomplish this, the design utilises photochromic glass and external shading devices, activated by a network of processing units linked to environmental sensors.

Response to wind

The wind forces are to be rationalised by active wind deflection shields, controlled by a neural network. These will deflect to the wind flow as and where necessary to avoid resonant turbulence, and will also reduce the lateral drag force by increasing surface roughness when required.

In the past, skyscrapers have been seen merely as glamorous observation platforms; now they may be reborn as climatic moderators – civil engineering infrastructures supporting life and work.

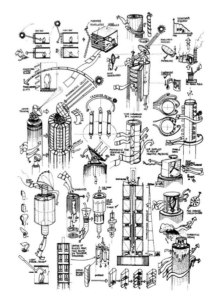

fig 84 Concept sketches for ventilation strategy for tower.

BEDALES THEATRE

Hampshire, UK

Situated in the rolling countryside of Hampshire, Bedales Theatre has an unseasoned oak structure with walls and roof of treated larch boards. Essentially a pyramid on a plinth, it seats up to 300 people. Form, plan, choice of materials and services all convey a straightforward, humane approach. The overall height is 18 metres, with a total floor area (including balconies, foyer, workshop etc) of 687 square metres.

Avoidance of air-conditioning, with its high energy consumption and dependence on CFCs or more commonly HCFCs, was mandatory.

Ventilation strategy

A slightly sloping site was a gift to the design team: air could easily be introduced into the building below floor level. A second important advantage of the site was that noise does not pose a problem; it was agreed with the client that the occasional plane flying overhead would not be disruptive.

Theatres are characterised by high loadings from audiences and, intermittently, from stage lighting. Approximately 50 per cent of the energy consumed by the stage lighting is a heat load to the occupied space. In the case of Bedales, calculations were based on loadings of approximately 100 W/m2 from people and 20 W/m2 from lighting.

A goal was set to try to ensure that the peak internal temperature did not exceed the peak external temperature by more than 3°C. The key issue then became one of how to design the building to incorporate thermal mass, where possible, and to ensure that the ventilation paths were sufficient and worked with the mass.

fig 86 Exterior of theatre.

fig 85 (opposite) Interior of theatre.

fig 87 View of access platform and Punkah fan.

Thermal mass was most easily incorporated in the plinth, which took the form of a concrete base with blockwork walls. The timber pyramidal structure has only moderate mass (the roof admittance is 2.3 Wm2K).

The ample open areas for inlet and outlet air are, respectively, 5 and 6 per cent of the floor area. Air flows straight through the building, entering at low level and passing underneath the seats, then rising through the theatre, past a high-level steel access platform and out through the top.

Heat recovery would neither have been very practical, nor economical, the main problem with occupied theatres being an excess of heat rather than a deficit. A carbon-dioxide sensor at high level ensures sufficient fresh air. If additional air is required for cooling, temperature sensors cause motorised inlet dampers and outlet panels to open, providing that doing so will result in a lowering of the internal temperature. A simple but elegant Punkah fan can be brought on to assist flow if required. Using this system, the building can be cooled at night to lower its temperature in preparation for a performance the next day.

Partial monitoring of conditions under a heat-load test indicated that throughout almost all of the occupied zone, temperatures were within the 3°C target set. These would have been lower if it had proved possible to incorporate more thermal mass, thus re-emphasising the importance of this aspect of the design.

Bedales is the first theatre to have been specifically designed for assisted natural ventilation with its modern use of controls and integration with the building fabric and form.

SUMMARY DATA

Client
Bedales School Theatre

Location
Hampshire, UK

Design Consortium
Feilden Clegg Architects, Roderick James Architect, Carpenter Oak Woodland Co

Structural Engineer
Ian Duncan

Services Engineer
Max Fordham Associates

Client Project Manager
Sir Hugh Beach, Tim Battle

Client Construction Manager
Paul Buxey

Fire Engineer
Buro Happold

Mechanical Contractor
Corrall-Montenay

Electrical Contractor
Southern Electrical Contracting

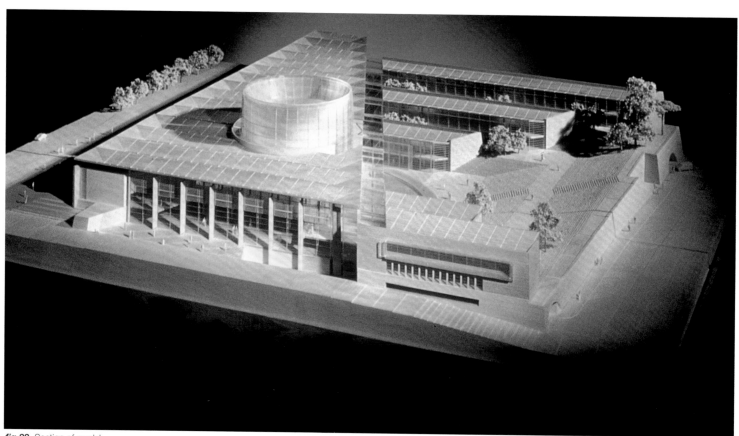

fig 88 Section of model.

HOUSE OF REPRESENTATIVES PARLIAMENT BUILDING

Nicosia, Cyprus

The competition-winning scheme consists of three main blocks:
- assembly hall
- foyer space
- offices.

Temperatures in Nicosia can be as high as 47°C during mid-summer, and air-conditioning is therefore essential to provide comfort. However, in spring and autumn maximum temperatures are 30 to 35°C, with night-time lows of 10 to 15°C. Due to the extremity of these temperature variations between night and day (15–20°C) it is possible, by using controlled night-time ventilation, to achieve a day-time temperature that represents the average between night and day – ie 20 to 25°C.

The foyer consists of a large, internal space enclosed by a precast concrete roof and perimeter glazing to provide views of the internal courtyard from one side and external views from the other. The wind was a crucial element in driving the ventilation system, utilised through wind towers positioned around the assembly hall, drawing air through the building from perimeter vents on the shaded courtyard facade. At night, cool air is drawn through the foyer by the wind towers from the secure grilles. The exposed concrete roof radiates heat to the air flow and cools down to act as a source of radiant cooling the next day. The roof is highly insulated to reduce heat gain and 'coolth' loss. The perimeter glazing is shaded by the roof overhang and facade louvres.

SUMMARY DATA

Client
Cyprus Government
User
Cyprus Government
Location
Nicosia, Cyprus
Architect
Kohn Pederson Fox and D Kythreotis and Partners
Structural Engineer
Battle McCarthy in collaboration with KAL
Building Services Engineer
Battle McCarthy in collaboration with UNIMEC
Environmental Engineer
Battle McCarthy

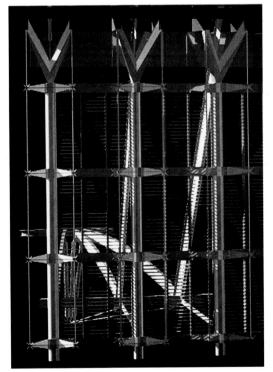

fig 89 Model of double skin.

EU PAVILION

Lisbon Expo 98, Portugal

The European Union required a roof-level canopy for the EU Pavilion to protect visitors to its VIP conference facilities from the elements without enclosing the terrace. The building is projected into the River Tagus and is therefore very much exposed to the prevailing winds. The challenge lay in generating an aerodynamic form that would moderate these extremes rather than eliminating the experience of being outside.

A number of design options were modelled. The preference was for a fabric roof that would extend beyond the footprint of the building to provide the necessary weather protection to the perimeter deck. The internal assembly room/covered courtyard was enclosed by the perimeter meeting rooms. Air was drawn from beneath the perimeter meeting rooms and out through six wind towers.

The space-frame structure created two layers of fabric: a lower ceiling and a high-level canopy. Wind towers were created by the branched structure supporting the canopy. Air flow through the covered courtyard was controlled by the air intake beneath the perimeter meeting blocks.

For the first time, comparable form-finding exercises were carried out, whereby the ideal fabric-stress shape was cross-referenced to the ideal wind-draw shape. The analysis was repeated to find the appropriate stress and wind shape, which created a far more curved form than that of typical fabric structures.

SUMMARY DATA
Client
EU 98 Expo
Location
Lisbon Expo 98, Portugal
Architect
MICE/Ideias do Futuro
Environmental Engineer
Battle McCarthy

fig 90 CFD Model of roof.

RARE HEADQUARTERS

East Midlands, UK

Owner-occupier buildings such as the Rare Headquarters provide opportunities for developing high-quality environmental designs specifically for the occupiers' individual needs. Typically, headquarters buildings cost less than 1 per cent of the occupiers' operation costs, including salaries and expenses throughout the life of the building.

The project responds to the inventive nature of Rare's computer-games software business and to its prioritisation of low-energy design and the creative use of 'green' materials. In order to produce an environment in tune with individual workstations, the local environment for each is controlled by an air-conditioning system within the design of the desk.

The buildings use a daylit, natural/mechanical mixed-mode system. The general background area is naturally ventilated through perimeter, motorised, louvred vents, the air exiting through a wind 'ridge' rather than a tower, which was not appropriate for the linear, close-centre workstation arrangement.

Spaced apart, so that there is no interference between them, the creative blocks fan out from the administration blocks and are generally orthogonal to the prevailing southwesterly winds, ensuring the effectiveness of the ridge.

SUMMARY DATA

Client
Rare
Location
East Midlands, UK

Architect
Fielden Clegg Architects
Structures and Services Engineer
Battle McCarthy
Environmental Engineer
Battle McCarthy

fig 91

fig 92

fig 93

fig 94 Wind towers situated above atrium.

REGENTS PARK HEALTH CENTRE

London, UK

Doctors at the Regents Park Health Centre wanted a 'healthy' environment for their staff and patients, and good ventilation was therefore a priority. However, due to security considerations, it was not possible to rely solely on ventilation from windows. Wind towers provided the ideal design solution.

The building consists of three zones:

• waiting area/reception

• doctors' room

• basement daycare centre.

The original ventilation proposal for the waiting area was to pull air from the front door to the reception area. However, this would have drawn air over sick patients to the receptionist. To avoid this, the air was supplied from perimeter windows and went out through a wind tower located near the entrance of the waiting area.

The doctors' room has openable, slim windows with security grilles that double up as external shading. The daycare centre is supplied with air through a cool-earth chamber situated below the building, exhausted via the roof wind tower.

SUMMARY DATA
Client
Camden and Islington Health Authority
Location
Regents Park Estate, North London
Occupiers
Doctors
Architect
The Douglas Stephen Partnership Ltd
Structures and Services Engineer
Battle McCarthy
Environmental Engineer
Battle McCarthy

fig 95

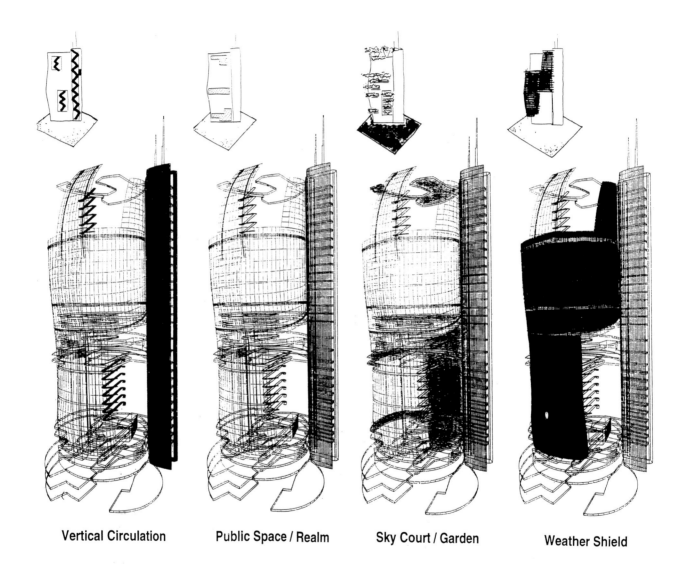

Vertical Circulation   **Public Space / Realm**   **Sky Court / Garden**   **Weather Shield**

fig 96

ARMOURY TOWER

Shanghai, China

The Armoury Tower consists of a series of accommodation blocks stacked on top of each other, including offices, retail, hotels and residential. Each block is separated by public sky gardens and a structure/service transfer zone.

The ventilation strategy for the blocks varies seasonally. In the summer, a wind scoop drops air down the central atria; this is then drawn out through the facades by the thermal flue enclosing the building form. In the winter, the wind scoop becomes a wind tower, drawing air from the building through the facades via solar collectors, which pre-heat it. During the mid-season period the building opens up and air is free to circulate around the building blocks through the sky gardens.

The tower has become a vertical segment of environmental buffer zones on a large scale, creating its own microclimate to suit the needs of its mixed tenure.

SUMMARY DATA

Client
Armoury Tower
Location
Shanghai, China
Architect
TR Hamzah and Yeang Sdn Bhd
Structures and Services Engineer
Battle McCarthy
Environmental Engineer
Battle McCarthy

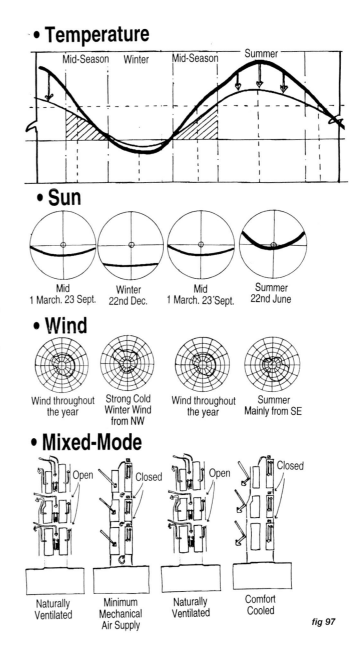

fig 97

fig 98 South-facing facade.

BRE ENVIRONMENTAL OFFICE

Watford, UK

The Building Research Establishment (BRE) site is surrounded by woodland on three sides, with the M1 on the remaining side. The new building is situated in the middle of the BRE, making its location semi-urban.

Deciding to practise what it preaches, the BRE commissioned a low-energy, environmentally friendly office. The intention was that it would be used as a showcase building and as a test bed for further research by BRE.

It consists of 1,250 square metres of offices on three floors, a large seminar room for 100 people and two smaller ones for 20 people. The office part of the building has concrete floor slabs on steel columns, a timber roof and brick-and-block walls. Recycled brick, concrete and flooring materials were used as part of the environmental approach.

Because of the low-energy targets, avoidance of air-conditioning was essential. However, the brief also specified internal summertime temperatures, which required an effective ventilation strategy.

The building is mainly ventilated using simple cross-ventilation. For this reason, the cross-section through the offices was kept below 14 metres. In order for the office layout to be as flexible as possible, however, it was designed to be partitioned up. The obvious place to do this was along the line of the corridor, where, unfortunately, the partitions would block the cross-ventilation.

To solve the problem, routeways had to be created so that the ventilation air could cross the cellular offices. This could have been done by running a duct either below the raised floor or above a false ceiling. If the air were taken below the floor it would not work well because any cooling effect from the concrete slab would tend to reduce the flow. If it were taken above a false ceiling, this would remove the radiant effect of the cooled concrete ceiling slab from the occupants of the building. The solution was to create air paths through the concrete slab itself.

In the winter, fresh air can be admitted through the high-level windows. This blows through the slab air duct, picking up some warmth, so that by the time it drops into the offices it is preheated.

In summer, air blows in through the high-level windows and picks up coolness stored in the slab during the previous night. It then drops down into the offices below. The slab will also radiate its stored cool thermal energy directly to the occupants of the offices. At night, the high-level windows will be opened to remove any excess heat that has built up during the previous day, and to cool down the concrete slab, which will store that coolness until the next day.

These solutions offered the architect a building with an interesting interior, the structural engineer a more efficient structure, and the services engineers an increased thermal mass as well as cross-ventilation air paths.

When there is no wind, the ventilation will be induced using stack-effect ventilation up stacks located on the south facade of the building. The stacks in the offices only connect the ground and first floors. This is because there is less height available above the second floor, so the stacks would not have been so effective. Low power (48W) propeller fans are mounted at high level in the stacks to provide additional drive in rare cases of temperature inversion in the stacks.

To ensure efficiency, a saltbath model was used to analyse air flows.

Generally, the site is fairly quiet, but the M1 does provide a steady background rumble over the entire site. Because of the need to isolate the seminar rooms from this external noise, these rooms are ventilated by stack effect alone. Additionally, acoustic panels were incorporated into the fresh-air inlets and stacks.

fig 99
Main Seminar Room showing ventilation tower.

fig 100
Internal view of offices showing translucent windows into stack and ventilation air paths through concrete ceiling slabs.

SUMMARY DATA

Client
Buildings Research Establishment (BRE)

Location
Watford, UK

Architect
Feilden Clegg Architects

Structural Engineer
Buro Happold

Services Engineer
Max Fordham and Partners

Project Manager
BWA Project Services

Quantity Surveyor
Turner and Townsend

Construction Manager
Symonds Travers Morgan Ltd

Main Contractor
John Sisk and Son Ltd

M&E Contractor
Norstead Services Ltd

fig 101 Haute Vallée School campus.

HAUTE VALLÉE SCHOOL THEATRE AND TEACHING BLOCK

Jersey, Channel Islands

This competition-winning scheme responded to a brief for a high-environmental, low-energy school. It consists of a cluster of buildings around a central square, each building type designed to fulfil its own particular environmental demands.

The scheme resulted in a range of low-energy designs for:

- offices
- classrooms
- theatres
- sports halls
- libraries
- laboratories
- studios
- workshops
- indoor swimming pools.

The winning entry gained the 'Jersey Environmental and Energy Vote' and received a substantial grant to pay for the environmental specialists, which included:

- *Energy* Exeter University Energy Research Unit
- *Daylight* Cambridge Architectural Research Ltd
- *Wind* University of Bristol, Department of Aero Engineering
- *CFD Analysis* Building Simulation Ltd
- *Acoustics* Arup Acoustics, Winchester.

Theatre

The ventilation concept for the theatre consists of bringing air in below the theatre floor and out through a central, high-level wind tower. Due to the ground conditions, the foundations were laid 1.5 metres below ground level with a suspended ground-floor slab. This structural solution provided a means of accessing air from beneath the building without incurring the extra cost of earth tubes.

Air is drawn through the theatre beneath the raised removable seating and out through the wind tower. Special care had to be taken in the design of the wind tower to ensure that sound ingress to, and escape from, the theatre was controlled to an acceptable standard for the required acoustic levels and for the comfort of neighbouring housing. The wind tower was subdivided and lagged with acoustic absorbing material without a major effect on the air flow from the building.

In addition, it was necessary to give special attention to the control of daylight for particular events. Within the theatre, a canopy was erected beneath the wind tower to blank out direct daylight without inhibiting the air flow. The daylight shield also acted as an acoustic absorber and as the support for the lighting.

Teaching blocks

The single-aspect teaching blocks form a crescent to the playing fields. They are south-facing in order to optimise solar gain as well as to take advantage of the view towards the coast. Two storeys high, they reduce the built area and thus provide more playing space. They also concur with the natural fall of the site, which steps down to the playing fields, making the first floor accessible directly from the square.

Although the first floor could have been naturally ventilated with openable windows, the ground floor, enclosed by the rear corridor, did not have the means of cross-ventilation. To solve this, wind towers were designed on the party walls between teaching blocks to draw air from both floors. These became the main structural service columns that support and stabilise the building, allowing for more slender props on the elevation.

To ensure that acoustic isolation between teaching blocks was maintained, and that there was fire separation between floors, each of the air paths was isolated and acoustic attenuation was provided.

The wind towers provide a reliable method of ventilation and of drawing controllable cross-ventilation on summer nights to provide night-time cooling. For security reasons, the windows are closed at night, but low-level grilles may be left open, through which air is drawn by the wind towers. As the cool night air passes through the building, the exposed concrete slabs and roofs re-radiate the heat gained in the day. By morning, the cool, exposed concrete provides radiant cooling.

This dependable system has proved to be an important asset to the school, especially for the hiring-out of classrooms during the holidays for commercial seminars.

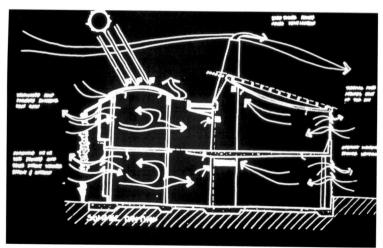

fig 102 Teaching-block ventilation strategy.

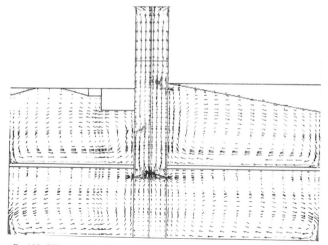

fig 103 CFD-analysis wind towers provide controllable natural ventilation.

fig 104 Haute Vallée School, south facade.

SUMMARY DATA

Client
Haute Vallée School

Location
Jersey, Channel Islands

Architect
PLB Architecture, Winchester

Structures and Services Engineer
Battle McCarthy Jersey in collaboration
with RWI

Environmental Engineer
Battle McCarthy Jersey

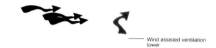

fig 105a

Wind assisted ventilation tower

Heat recovery ventilation plant

Additional air inlet via atrium doors in summer

Controlled air inlet

Air supply through raised floor

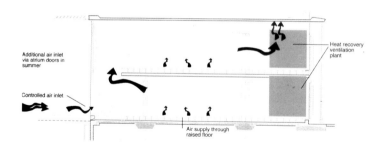

fig 105b

Air via toilets

Heat recovery cooling plant

Raised floor supply

Air via toilets

Raised floor supply

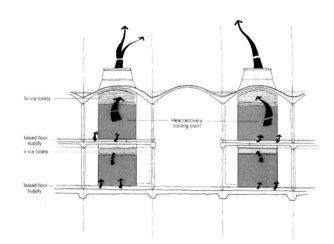

fig 105c

Mini atrium

Office

Street

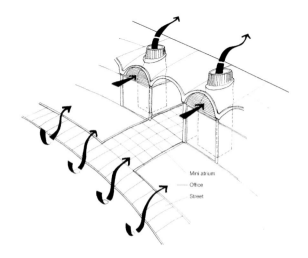

figs 105a, b, c Fresh air is supplied into the building under the curtain wall, and air is then extracted via the wind towers.

PILKINGTON GLASS HEADQUARTERS

St Helens, UK

The Pilkington Glass Headquarters provided the design team with the opportunity to create a high-environmental quality, low-energy landmark building. Constructed on an asymmetric plan, it is glazed towards the south, with shading and light shelves. Towards the back of the linear block a series of wind towers combines with the primary service cores.

The buildings utilise mixed-mode natural/mechanical ventilation. During the winter and mid-season periods, fresh air is drawn through low-level grilles in the facade. The rooms are designed with deep floor-to-ceiling heights to allow for thermal stratification. Exposed, precast concrete slabs act as a thermal mass for night-time cooling, and compensate for temperature fluctuations in day-time.

The wind towers provide the necessary draw to remove the extract air throughout the day and at night. Constructed in glass, they also act as thermal draughts: the sun's rays pass through them and are absorbed by internal louvres that heat the air. As the temperature rises, the density of the air falls, and the air ascends. As it does so, it draws air from below through the building.

SUMMARY DATA

Client
Pilkington Glass Ltd

Location
St Helens, UK

Architect
Richard Rogers and Partners

Environmental Engineer
Battle McCarthy

fig 106
Umno Tower, north-west facade

UMNO TOWER

Penang, Malaysia

The UMNO Tower is situated in the centre of Georgetown, Penang. Of its 21 storeys, 14 are offices; it also contains a space for a banking hall and auditoriums.

The external climate in Malaysia is humid, with little seasonal or diurnal variation. Modern buildings in noisy, polluted city locations – especially offices, with their additional internal heat load from lighting, machines and people – tend to be designed entirely to reject the external climate, relying on air-conditioning and artificial lighting. UMNO does encompass artificial air-conditioning, but it can also be naturally ventilated if conditions are suitable.

Wind is used as a source of fresh-air supply to the interior, and to create comfort inside the building. For internal comfort, a higher level of air change per hour is required. A series of wing walls is therefore orientated to catch the prevailing wind.

These are simply short walls, placed perpendicular to the inlet leading to the building's interior, which are used in combination with the opening as a pocket-like device to collect and direct the prevailing winds into the building. Attached to a balcony device with full-height sliding doors, they enhance internal comfort conditions through air changes, temperature and humidity. The placement of the wing walls and air locks within the floor plate are based on the architect's assessment of the locality's wind data.

The building maximises the use of daylight so that its occupants can enjoy natural light, and to reduce energy use and heat emissions. All office

Wind-flow around building (vertical section) in the form of air pressure contours

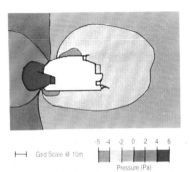

Wind-flow around the building (Level 12) in the form of air pressure contours

fig 107 Wind-flow around building (vertical section) in form of air pressure contours.

fig 108 Wind-flow around building (Level 12) in form of air pressure contours.

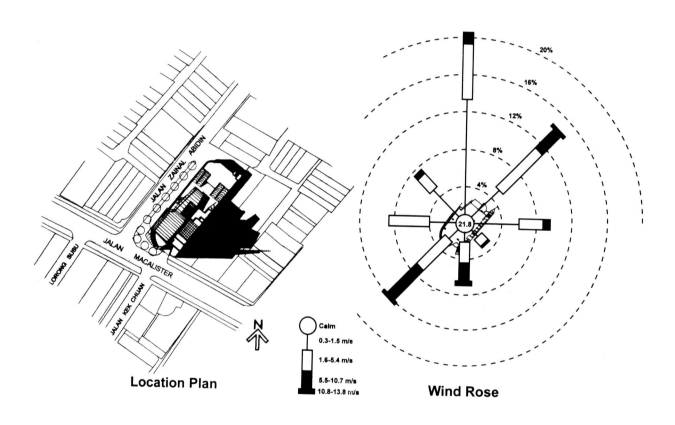

Location Plan

Wind Rose

Calm
0.3-1.5 m/s
1.6-5.4 m/s
5.5-10.7 m/s
10.8-13.8 m/s

fig 109
Wind pressure analysis diagrams

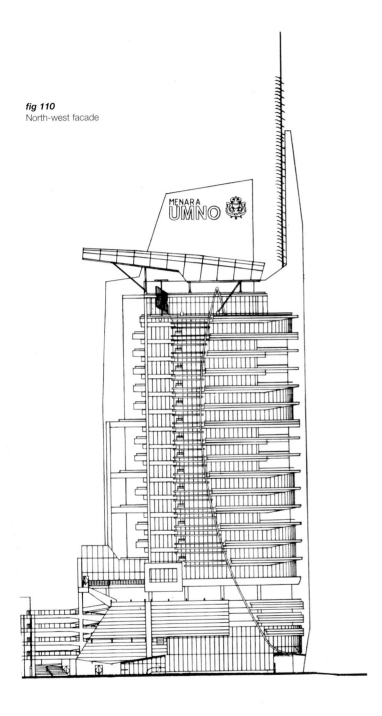

fig 110
North-west facade

floors can be naturally ventilated and no desk is located more than 6.5 metres from an openable window. Solar shading lessens the impact of heat gain, and windows and balcony doors are adjustable to control the wind-induced ventilation. The building is situated on an open site with no interference from other high-rise structures. Natural ventilation is introduced at point of entry (rather than creating suction at the leeward side).

All lift lobbies, staircases and lavatories have natural sunlight and ventilation, not only making the building low energy, but also rendering it safer in the event of power failure or other emergencies.

SUMMARY DATA

Client
*South East Asia Development
Corporation Bhd*

Location
Jalan Macalister, Penang, Malaysia

Architect
TR Hamzah & Yeang Sdn Bhd

C & S Engineer
Tahir Wong Sdn Bhd

M & E Engineer
Ranhill Bersekutu Sdn Bhd

Concept Engineer
Battle McCarthy

FURTHER READING

Historical Precedent Studies – Middle East

Bookhhash, Fuad M, 'Wind Tower Houses of Bastakeya in Dubai'

Fahty, Hassan, *Architecture for the Poor*, University of Chicago Press (Chicago), 1973

Fahty, Hassan, *Natural Energy and the Vernacular Architecture*

Gurdil, Fatme I/Memecan, Salih/Turan, Mete, 'Passive Cooling in Mardin – A Vernacualr Solution in Hot-Arid Regions'

Roaf, Susan, 'The Traditional Technology Trap, Stereotypes of Middle Eastern Traditional Building Types and Technologies'

Rudofsky, Bernard, *Architecture without Architects*, Academy Editions (London), 1964

Rudofsky, Bernard, *The Prodigious Builders*, Secker and Warburg (London), 1977

Historical Precedent Studies – Tropical Examples

Lim Jee Yuan, *The Malay House*, Institute Masyarakat

Historical Precedent Studies – Temperate Examples

Banham, Reyner, *The Architecture of the Well-Tempered Environment*, University of Chicago Press (Chicago), 1969

Boswell Reid, David, *Illustrations of the Theory and Practice of Natural Ventilation*, 1872

Environmental Design

Harrington-Lynn, L/Milbank, NO/Petherbridge, P, *Environmental Design Manual – Summer Conditions in Naturally Ventilated Offices*, British Research Establishment Report, 1988

Irving, Steve/Uys, Eugene, *CIBSE Design and Application Manual*

Lechner, Norbert, *Heating, Cooling, Lighting – Design Methods for Architects*, John Wiley & Sons Ltd (Chichester), 1991

Lundtang Peterson, Erik/Troen, Ib, *European Wind Atlas*, Riso National Laboratory (Roskilde)

Martin, AJ, *Control of Natural Ventilation*, BSRIA, 1995

Parkyn, 'Naturally does it', *ABCD*, October 1995

Szokolay, SV, *Environmental Science Handbook*, The Construction Press, 1980

Woodward, Antony, 'Windows of Opportunity', *Perspectives*, April 1995

'Cambridge Calling', *The Architects Journal* (London), 1 December 1994

'Tax Haven', *Building* (London), 28 October 1994

'Aerodynamic Design', Centre Scientific et Technique du Batiment'

ACKNOWLEDGEMENTS

Christopher McCarthy and Guy Battle wish to acknowledge Tom Lawson's pioneering wind design of our built environment. Without his determination and commitment, wind-driven ventilation would still be merely a concept buried in the past. We also wish to thank the clients, architects, engineers, quantity surveyors, environmental laboratories and contractors for their contribution in making the concept reality. Thanks also to our families for supporting our quest to understand the mystery of the interaction of natural forces with built form, in the year the Partnership celebrates its sixth birthday. Finally, we wish to thank the team who have contributed to the Partnership's first book.